Essentials of Writing

FOURTH EDITION

VINCENT F. HOPPER AND CEDRIC GALE

New York University

Fourth Edition Revised by

BENJAMIN W. GRIFFITH, JR.

West Georgia College

BARRON'S EDUCATIONAL SERIES, INC.

All inquiries should be addressed to:
Barron's Educational Series, Inc.
250 Wireless Boulevard
Hauppauge, New York 11788

Library of Congress Catalog Card Number 90–25418
International Standard Book No. 0-8120-4630-7

PRINTED IN THE UNITED STATES OF AMERICA

123   100   98765432

CONTENTS

HOW TO USE THIS BOOK

As in the earlier editions, published under the title of *Practice for Effective Writing*, this series of exercises in grammar and composition may be used independently or in conjunction with *Essentials of English*. When the two books are used together, the student should read a section of *Essentials of English*, then work on the corresponding exercise in this volume. Whenever he feels uncertain, he should refer back to the basic text. By reading, practicing, and testing immediately his comprehension of what he has read, the student is made secure in his knowledge of each step of what should be steady and solid progress toward the mastery of writing skill. Only by practice can confidence and expertness be assured.

In the ideal course the student should be assigned a section in the manual for study together with the corresponding exercise for practice. The exercises may be corrected by the instructor or by the students themselves through an exchange of papers in class. Most of the exercises require the students to do only one or two things. Usually, the answers are to be written in columns on the right-hand side of the page where they can be rapidly checked by the grader. The answers to be indicated within the text itself have been kept to a minimum and usually require only one kind of mark, such as parentheses, which can be easily spotted. Most of the exercises are presented in units of ten, twenty, twenty-five, or fifty for ease of scoring.

Since there are two or more sets of exercises for the more important principles, one of the sets and also the review exercises may be used as tests, if the instructor so desires. Or the instructor may reserve some of the exercises for students who require further study and practice in specific areas. For example, the instructor may suggest an improvement in a theme and then require the student to restudy the appropriate section in *Essentials of English* and do an additional exercise in *Essentials of Writing*.

The ability to write well comes naturally to few. It can be mastered, however, by conscientious study of *Essentials of English* and a great deal of systematic practice as provided for in *Essentials of Writing*.

CORRELATION OF EXERCISES
to sections of *Essentials of English*

1 IDENTIFYING NOUNS

Section 1A, *Essentials of English*

Two words are italicized in each of the following sentences. One of the two is a noun; the other is not. Identify the noun and write it in the space provided at the right.

EXAMPLE:

Mary scolded her brother *for* his bad *language*.   language

1. That *was* the *year* the Mets won the World Series. _____

2. *Marriage* is *like* a supermarket: easy to get into but hard to get out of. _____

3. The moon might be a nice *place* to visit but I wouldn't want to live *there*. _____

4. People's opinions are *not* always the *result* of their experience. _____

5. The New York Knicks showed *that* basketball could be an *art* as well as a game. _____

6. Having been bitten by a large collie when he was a child, he was never *able* to conquer his *fear* of dogs. _____

7. The *store* was closed when I *got* there. _____

8. He was *afraid* of *policemen* when he was little. _____

9. Part of one's earnings should be *given* to *charity*. _____

10. The *entire* *nation* mourned the death of Martin Luther King, Jr. _____

11. As a *girl* she was very *shy*, but she got over that when she grew older. _____

12. According to a Spanish proverb, a woman's *advice* isn't worth much, *but* he who doesn't take it is a *fool*. _____

13. Christopher Morley *said* that *life* should be made up of learning, earning, and yearning. _____

14. *Without* crime, sports, and comics, many newspapers would go out of *business*. _____

15. *Thousands* of adults attend evening classes and take correspondence courses in subjects *which* they never studied in school.

_____

16. Science has produced *comforts,* but *also* pollution.

_____

17. The new secretary takes *dictation* very slowly, but her typing leaves nothing to be *desired.*

_____

18. Common *sense* is *frequently* a good substitute for elaborate theories.

_____

19. The jury reached a *verdict very* quickly.

_____

20. *All* of the *signers* of the Declaration of Independence were relatively young men.

_____

21. Good health is a *valuable* asset to any kind of *work*

_____

22. Never *seek trouble* until trouble troubles you.

_____

23. My friend's partner *danced* the last *dance* with me.

_____

24. The plumber was using a large *wrench* when he *wrenched* his arm.

_____

25. Farmers have always *worked* hard in the spring whether they enjoyed their *work* or not.

_____

2 IDENTIFYING NOUNS

Section 1A, *Essentials of English*

Each of the following sentences contains only two nouns. Identify the nouns and write them in the spaces at the right in the order in which they appear in the sentences.

EXAMPLE:

Every dog has its day.   dog   day

1. Traffic was extremely heavy in the city.

2. The roads were paved with concrete.

3. Since he was late, John gulped down his breakfast without even sitting down.

4. Haste makes waste.

5. Never again in their whole lives were they to have such a frightening experience.

6. Mary was as noble and kind as her brother was selfish and cruel.

7. Please turn off the lights before you leave the room.

8. The exits were all illuminated so that they could be easily seen by everybody sitting in the auditorium.

9. The noise made by the children playing nearby was very irritating.

10. The books were tied together and piled outside in the corridor.

11. It seemed to him that he had never before taken so long to finish an assignment that was only five pages long.

12. After riding for hours on a hot, dirty, crowded bus, he finally realized that he was not as eager to go away as he thought he had been.

13. There are a great many good programs on television, but you have to know where to look for them.

_____ _____

14. The personality of the young actor made him very popular.

_____ _____

15. John begged his father to let him go away.

_____ _____

16. He ate two hot dogs at a nearby lunchroom before he got too hungry.

_____ _____

17. The gathering mists of night made it necessary to pack up and leave as soon as possible.

_____ _____

18. Only those who have a great deal of strength and who are willing to work hard will be selected.

_____ _____

19. The teacher dismissed the class before she should have.

_____ _____

20. The child was racing down the street so rapidly that it seemed as if he would never be able to stop himself.

_____ _____

21. A friend is a person who knows all about you and likes you anyway.

_____ _____

22. It is surprising to realize that many good students get poor grades because they don't know how to study.

_____ _____

23. He never drove his car because he was afraid that he would lose his parking place.

_____ _____

24. What he was reading seemed so dull that he closed the book and threw it on the floor.

_____ _____

25. If this assignment seems stupid because it is so easy, you are progressing rapidly on basic writing tools.

_____ _____

3 IDENTIFYING AND CAPITALIZING PROPER NOUNS

Section 1B, *Essentials of English*

Each of the following sentences contains one or more words that should be capitalized. Identify these proper nouns (or adjectives derived from proper nouns) and write them with correct capitalization in the spaces provided at the right.

EXAMPLE:

He lived in columbus, ohio.   **Columbus, Ohio**

1. She went west with her aunt louise.

2. Her aunt had always lived in the west.

3. It was the warmest sunday of the summer.

4. He attended a high school in new england.

5. The quakers in town were very religious.

6. He has been working after school and on weekends at that new restaurant, the purple cow.

7. I'll ask my mother if she will give me a novel by kurt vonnegut for graduation.

8. I'm not sure that mother will be willing to do it.

9. My father was born in italy.

10. He speaks very good english for a foreigner.

11. Our priest, father wilson, is a remarkable man.

12. I'll ask the doctor to come, even if it is christmas.

13. They ate at a hot dog stand before going to the orpheum theatre to see a movie.

14. Many mexicans have been moving north. _____

15. The largest building in the state is situated in chicago. _____

16. He became very fond of german sausages while he was studying abroad. _____

17. The boy begged his aunt to keep it a secret from the fellows on fourteenth street. _____

18. They called the play "the outcasts of the valley." _____

19. They dedicated the town hall on the fourth of july. _____

20. He studied history, economics, and a course entitled social institutions. _____

21. There are many public libraries in new york city. _____

22. Hundreds of children have been graduated from thomas jefferson high school. _____

23. His essay was entitled "the rewards of honesty." _____

24. Even though he has retired, he is still called judge wilson. _____

25. The secretary said, "mr. president, a visitor is waiting to see you." _____

4 POSSESSIVE CASE OF NOUNS

Sections 1D and 1E, *Essentials of English*

A possessive relationship is indicated in each of the following by the use of the words *belonging to*. Whenever it is correct to do so, rewrite the phrase using the possessive case with an apostrophe. When the use of the apostrophe is incorrect, rewrite the phrase using the preposition *of*.

EXAMPLES:

The hat belonging to John   John's hat _____

The roof belonging to the house   The roof of the house _____

1. The dress belonging to the woman _____

2. The club belonging to the women _____

3. The broom belonging to the janitor _____

4. The room belonging to the janitors _____

5. The novel belonging to Hughes _____

6. The chair belonging to the secretary _____

7. The suite belonging to the bosses _____

8. The mast belonging to the ship _____

9. The floor belonging to the room _____

10. The gyroscope belonging to the airplane _____

11. The essay belonging to John Abrams _____

12. The canoe belonging to Dick and John _____

13. The sweater belonging to Dick and the sweater belonging to John

_____

14. The works belonging to Shakespeare

_____

15. The house belonging to the Smiths

_____

16. The rails belonging to the fence

_____

17. The firm belonging to Salter, Stone, and Atlas

_____

18. The firms belonging individually to Salter, Stone, and Atlas

_____

19. The books belonging to Amos

_____

20. The ring belonging to John's mother-in-law

_____

In each of the following, replace the *of*-phrase with the idiomatic expression using the apostrophe.

EXAMPLE:

work of a day   **a day's work**

_____

21. a tour of three weeks

_____

22. worth of seven dollars

_____

23. time of one hour

_____

24. a vacation of two months

_____

25. worth of his money

_____

5 IDENTIFYING ANTECEDENTS OF PRONOUNS

Section 2, *Essentials of English*

A pronoun is italicized in each of the following sentences. Write the antecedent or antecedents of the pronoun in the space provided at the right.

EXAMPLE:

Mary looked like *her* sister.   Mary
_____

1. The senator was happy because *he* was re-elected.
_____

2. Be sure to put a stamp on the letter before mailing *it*.
_____

3. Frederick lost *his* jacket.
_____

4. The men wrote regularly to *their* wives.
_____

5. The children didn't get as many presents as *they* wanted.
_____

6. "*You* shouldn't do that," said Mr. Johnson to his young daughter.
_____

7. Money has no real value in *itself*.
_____

8. The man *who* works hard deserves to succeed.
_____

9. The mayor was angry at the people *who* had campaigned against him.
_____

10. The United Nations celebrated *its* thirty-fifth anniversary in October, 1980.
_____

11. The plants *that* were planted in the sun doubled their growth in a month.
_____

12. Mr. and Mrs. Johnson were very angry with *their* children.
_____

13. Nobody *who* is talented likes to be ignored.
_____

14. The love of books is a love *that* requires neither justification, nor apology, nor defense.

_____

15. The barrel was full of apples, twenty of *which* were rotten.

_____

16. We find it sometimes easier to be honest with others than with *ourselves*.

_____

17. She was one of those women *who* are never at a loss for words.

_____

18. Every adult should have a sense of responsibility for *his* actions.

_____

19. Either Jane or Louise left *her* pocketbook in the restaurant.

_____

20. The candidates *whom* I interviewed yesterday seemed very unsatisfactory.

_____

21. The United States had *its* first Afro-American newspaper when *Freedom* was founded in New York City.

_____

22. He left the books and papers exactly as they were when he first saw *them*.

_____

23. "*My* uncle, Mr. Habersham, is the president of a publishing company," boasted little Susan.

_____

24. The offensive linemen of the Jets were angry because *they* received so little recognition.

_____

25. Potatoes, *which* are not as fattening as some persons think, are rich in vitamins.

_____

6 PERSONAL PRONOUNS

Sections 2A and 2B, *Essentials of English*

Each of the following specifies a particular form of a personal pronoun. Write the pronoun indicated in the space provided at the right of each specification.

EXAMPLE:

Second Person, Singular (Number), Possessive Case   your OR yours

1. Third Person, Neuter Gender, Singular, Nominative Case _____

2. First Person, Plural, Nominative Case _____

3. Third Person, Feminine Gender, Singular, Nominative Case _____

4. First Person, Singular, Possessive Case _____

5. Second Person, Plural, Objective Case _____

6. First Person, Plural, Possessive Case _____

7. Third Person, Neuter Gender, Plural, Objective Case _____

8. First Person, Singular, Nominative Case _____

9. Second Person, Plural, Nominative Case _____

10. Third Person, Feminine Gender, Singular, Objective Case _____

11. Third Person, Masculine Gender, Plural, Nominative Case _____

12. First Person, Singular, Objective Case _____

13. Third Person, Masculine Gender, Singular, Nominative Case _____

14. Third Person, Neuter Gender, Singular, Possessive Case _____

15. First Person, Plural, Objective Case _____

16. Second Person, Singular, Possessive Case _____

17. Third Person, Masculine Gender, Singular, Possessive Case _____

18. Third Person, Neuter Gender, Singular, Objective Case _____

19. Third Person, Feminine Gender, Plural, Possessive Case _____

20. Third Person, Masculine Gender, Singular, Objective Case _____

21. Third Person, Feminine Gender, Singular, Possessive Case _____

Each of the following specifies a particular form of the relative pronoun *who*. Write the pronoun indicated in the space provided at the right of each specification.

EXAMPLE:
Singular (Number), Nominative Case **who** _____

22. Plural, Nominative Case _____

23. Singular, Objective Case _____

24. Plural, Possessive Case _____

25. Singular, Possessive Case _____

7 IDENTIFYING VERBS

Section 3, *Essentials of English*

Two words are italicized in each of the following sentences. One of the two is a finite verb; the other is not. Identify the verb and write it in the space provided at the right.

EXAMPLE:

The family *ate* dinner *in* the restaurant.   ate

1. James A. Nealy *was* America's *first* Catholic bishop.   _____

2. He *devoted* most of his *evening* to study.   _____

3. *Crowds* of people *waited* restlessly at the airport.   _____

4. It *is* too late to do anything *about* it.   _____

5. About 5,000 *free* blacks *fought* in the American Revolution.   _____

6. She always *sings* her favorite *song*.   _____

7. Many ethnic groups *live* in the *continental* United States.   _____

8. Some *teachers teach* many different subjects.   _____

9. He *meets* his friends at the club *meetings*.   _____

10. The *cheering lasted* for a good twenty minutes.   _____

Some of the finite verbs in the following sentences include auxiliaries and some do not. Write the complete finite verb in each sentence in the space to the right.

EXAMPLE:

My brother is always complaining about trifles
<u>   is complaining   </u>

11. The storm finally blew itself out.

12. The wind had been blowing all night long.

13. Magazines will seldom print lengthy articles.

14. He expected to finish the job before evening.

15. I have been waiting for you for a long time.

16. He was resting after his strenuous activity.

17. We will doubtless be seeing him again.

18. The sun is setting in the west.

19. The dying man gasped for breath.

20. What can you expect of a man like that?

21. She will have completed the assignment by noon.

22. The money was spent recklessly and carelessly.

23. Congress has passed a bill prohibiting any discrimination in housing.

24. Playing basketball was his favorite form of recreation.

25. I do congratulate you on your well-deserved promotion.

8 TRANSITIVE AND INTRANSITIVE VERBS; VOICE AND MOOD OF VERBS

Sections 3C, 3D, and 3E, *Essentials of English*

In the first space provided at the right, state whether the verb italicized in each of the following sentences is transitive or intransitive, using the abbrevations *v. t.* and *v. i.* In the second space write the direct object of the verb if there is one.

	Verb	*Object*
EXAMPLES:		
I *walked* down the street.	v. i.	
The town *paved* the street.	v. t.	street

1. He *wrote* in his notebook. _____ _____
2. They *went* home early that night. _____ _____
3. The food *smelled* good. _____ _____
4. The dog *smelled* the bone in the bag. _____ _____
5. He *wrote* a report for the school board. _____ _____
6. Mr. Smith *was* a trustee of the college. _____ _____
7. He *had* plenty of money. _____ _____
8. The groom *said*, "I do." _____ _____
9. The preacher *spoke* too long. _____ _____
10. He *waited* several days for the message. _____ _____

In the space provided at the right, state whether each of the transitive verbs italicized in the following sentences is in the active or passive voice.

	Voice
EXAMPLES:	
John *hit* the ball.	active
The ball *was hit* by John.	passive

11. My mother *was blamed* for burning the biscuits. _____

12. The telephone pole *was struck* by lightning. _____

13. The food *was* all *eaten* before I got there. _____

14. Few actors *have been praised* by all the critics. _____

15. "Don't wait for me," *said* the driver. _____

16. *Give* me the best tickets you have. _____

17. The house *was burned* to the ground. _____

18. I *do* my best work in the morning. _____

In the space provided at the right, state whether the verb italicized in each of the following sentences is in the indicative, imperative, or subjunctive mood.

EXAMPLE: *Mood*

I wish I *were* home.   subjunctive
                                            _____

19. Please *pass* the butter. _____

20. *Will* you *wait* for me? _____

21. I suggested that he *look* for a job. _____

22. It looks as if it *will rain* before night. _____

23. If I *were* rich, I'd buy a new car. _____

24. *Send* me two dozen tennis balls. _____

25. I move that the motion *be* adopted. _____

9 CORRECT VERB FORMS

Sections 3F, 3H, 3I, 3J, 3K, *Essentials of English*

In each of the following sentences, a particular form of a given verb is designated in parentheses. Supply the form specified in the space provided at the right.

EXAMPLES:

Tomorrow I (future tense of *to mail*) the letter.   shall mail

The Indians (past tense, progressive form of *to live*) in tepees.   were living

1. Yesterday I (past tense of *to eat*) downtown.   _____

2. Tomorrow I (future tense of *to take*) the book to the library.   _____

3. She (past tense, progressive form of *to wash*) her hair when the doorbell rang.   _____

4. They (future tense, progressive form of *to see*) a great deal of each other next month.   _____

5. Harvard University (past tense of *to be*) the first college in America.   _____

6. They (past perfect tense of *to reach*) their destination before we got home from the airport.   _____

7. I (past perfect tense of *to hope*) that the postman would come before I had to leave the house.   _____

8. The club (present tense of *to meet*) every Wednes- at The Village Inn.   _____

9. A certified public accountant (present tense of *to audit*) the books of the company every year.   _____

10. The children (present perfect tense, progressive form of *to play*) in the yard ever since breakfast.   _____

11. He (past perfect tense, progressive form of *to wait*) for an hour before she arrived.   _____

12. By dinner time I (future perfect tense of *to mend*) all of the torn clothes.   _____

13. The workmen (present tense, progressive form of *to put*) a new roof on the building.

_____

14. From now on, you (future tense of *to do,* indicating a command) whatever you are told.

_____

15. By next September, the army (future perfect tense, progressive form of *to fight*) for six months.

_____

16. The campers (future tense of *to leave*) for home at the first sign of cold weather.

_____

17. The sailors (past perfect tense, progressive form of *to expect*) letters from home when they reached port, but they were disappointed.

_____

18. I (future tense of *to attend,* indicating a promise) every meeting of the committee if I can possibly do so.

_____

19. Hemingway (present tense of *to write*) in a deceptively simple style.

_____

20. We (present perfect tense, progressive form of *to plan*) to go to Canada for several years.

_____

10 CORRECT FORMS OF IRREGULAR VERBS

Principal Parts of Irregular Verbs, *Essentials of English*

In each of the following sentences, the infinitive of an irregular verb is placed in parentheses. In the space provided write the correct form required by the context of the sentence.

EXAMPLE:

I have (to bring) a friend home for dinner.   brought

1. The United Nations (to bid) the nation to desist from further aggression after complaints had been received.

2. In colonial days parents (to beat) their children regularly.

3. He has (to bear) his burden of grief for many years.

4. The river rose so high that it (to burst) through the dikes.

5. He has (to cast) off all his bad habits.

6. When I was offered only two flavors of ice cream, I (to choose) vanilla.

7. After his friend died, he (to cling) to every precious memory of the past.

8. I'll be ready to play as soon as you have (to deal) the cards.

9. Even though the water was icy, he (to dive) into the lake without hesitating.

10. The children have eaten their sandwiches and (to drink) their milk.

11. When a price was put on his head, he (to flee) from the country.

12. The planes rose to a high altitude and (to fly) in intricate formations.

13. The captain became reckless and (to fling) discretion to the winds.

14. I have (to forbid) him to come to the house again.

_____

15. They washed the blankets and (to hang) them on the line to dry.

_____

16. He was convicted of murder and (to hang) in the public square.

_____

17. When the organ stopped playing, the bride and groom (to kneel) at the altar.

_____

18. The shepherd rounded up the sheep and (to lead) them to a new pasture.

_____

19. It would have been a home run if the fielder had not (to leap) high in the air to catch the ball.

_____

20. I shall (to lie) in the hammock and rest awhile.

_____

21. They were (to lay) the rug in the living room.

_____

22. The old rug had (to lie) there for years.

_____

23. The papers were (to lie) all over the table.

_____

24. He picked up his books and (to lay) them on the desk.

_____

25. She stretched out on the sand and (to lie) on the beach all afternoon.

_____

11 CORRECT FORMS OF IRREGULAR VERBS

Principal Parts of Irregular Verbs, *Essentials of English*

In each of the following sentences, the infinitive of an irregular verb is placed in parentheses. Write the correct form required by the context of the sentence in the space provided at the right.

EXAMPLE:

I have (to teach) him everything I know. _____taught_____

1. The sun had (to rise) before we reached our destination. _____

2. He discovered that his car had (to run) out of gasoline. _____

3. After being reprimanded for her misbehavior, she (to seek) to mend her ways. _____

4. They had (to set) up the card tables and were ready to play. _____

5. As you can see from here, the house (to sit) on the very top of the hill. _____

6. The tables had all been (to set) for dinner. _____

7. The missile has (to sit) on its launching pad ever since it arrived at the base. _____

8. The cruiser (to sink) before the coast guard could reach it. _____

9. Twenty of the settlers had been (to slay) by the natives. _____

10. He picked up a stone and (to sling) it over the fence. _____

11. The dog put its tail between its legs and (to slink) out of sight. _____

12. If he had not (to speak), I would have sworn that he was an American. _____

13. The bee buzzed about his head and (to sting) him on the cheek. _____

14. He opened the front door and (to stride) down the stairs.

_____

15. I could have (to swear) that I heard the clock strike.

_____

16. My mother dusted the furniture and (to sweep) the floor.

_____

17. The enemy had (to swim) across the river and attacked us from the rear.

_____

18. He raised the lantern and (to swing) it back and forth several times.

_____

19. The chickens had the best possible food and they (to thrive) on it.

_____

20. They have (to throw) out all the old furniture.

_____

21. No matter how hard I have tried to sleep during the morning, I have (to wake) up every day at seven o'clock.

_____

22. John has never (to wear) his new shoes.

_____

23. She (to weep) when she heard that her son was in prison.

_____

24. She put the mop in the pail of water and then (to wring) it out.

_____

25. Have you (to write) any letters to your congressman?

_____

12 IDENTIFYING ADJECTIVES

Sections 4A, 4B, 4C, *Essentials of English*

Two words are italicized in each of the following sentences. One of the two is an adjective; the other is not. Identify the adjective and write it in the first space provided at the right. In the second space, write the noun or pronoun which it modifies.

EXAMPLES:	ADJECTIVE	MODIFYING
She *rented* a *small* house.	small	house
I was *too sick* to eat.	sick	I

1. The *old* book *was* falling to pieces.

2. He *eagerly* accepted the check from *the* cashier.

3. Over half of both black and *white* Americans *graduate* from high school.

4. She quickly *slipped a* small bill from her wallet.

5. Hard work made him *very tired*.

6. *Lazy* or not, he managed to accomplish a great *deal*.

7. She had *an* orange for breakfast and a glass of milk *for* lunch.

8. The dog seemed *sick* after *eating* its dinner.

9. The picture, small *but beautiful*, brought a very low price at the sale.

10. His talk made *no* impression *at* all on the audience.

Each of the following sentences contains two adjectives. Identify the adjectives and write them in the spaces at the right in the order in which they occur in the sentence.

EXAMPLE:

The older brother was named John.   the _____   older _____

11. Bruce Dern is famous as an actor.   _____   _____

12. He sent twenty letters to friends of the family. _____   _____

13. I want to become rich and famous.   _____   _____

14. Man has been called a thinking animal.   _____   _____

15. Tell them to let me know whenever they are ready to be sensible about things.   _____   _____

16. Wool makes better clothing than cotton for cold weather.   _____   _____

17. Sensitive people hate to be laughed at when they make foolish mistakes.   _____   _____

18. All intrinsic values can not be priced in terms of dollars and cents.   _____   _____

19. He put on an old hat and departed as quickly as he had come.   _____   _____

20. She felt miserable when she was told that nobody had called that day to congratulate her.   _____   _____

21. Tired and hungry, we trudged homeward in torrents of rain.   _____   _____

22. Problems can be simple if you know enough algebra to solve them.   _____   _____

23. Medieval armor was made of shining steel.   _____   _____

24. Skyscrapers could not be built without the use of steel beams.   _____   _____

25. John acted uncomfortable when he was told that he had been elected president of the fraternity.   _____   _____

13 IDENTIFYING ADVERBS

Section 4D, *Essentials of English*

An adverb is italicized in each of the following sentences. Write the word which the adverb modifies in the first space to the right of the sentence. In the second space, indicate whether the word modified is a verb, an adjective, or another adverb (using the conventional dictionary abbreviations for these parts of speech).

EXAMPLES:	*Word Modified*	*Part of Speech*
He ran *rapidly* to the window.	ran	v.
It was an *extremely* dull day.	dull	adj.
He ate *very* quickly.	quickly	adv.

1. I shall be *most* happy to come. _____ _____

2. The mother hummed *quietly* to her baby. _____ _____

3. The girls walked *home* in the rain. _____ _____

4. He *never* studied before examinations. _____ _____

5. He *hardly* ever did anything constructive. _____ _____

6. It was an *unusually* cold winter. _____ _____

7. *Quietly* they tiptoed into the room. _____ _____

8. The father waited *anxiously* for news of his son. _____ _____

9. They weren't *quite* ready to make the decision. _____ _____

10. Time goes very *fast* when one is busy. _____ _____

11. His wife is *really* pretty. _____ _____

Each of the following sentences contains two adverbs. Pick out the adverbs and write them in the spaces to the right in the order in which they occur.

EXAMPLE:

He left the room very quietly.　　　　　　　very　　　　　　　quietly

12. The maid finished her day's work and went home early.

13. The strawberries are hardly ever ripe before early June.

14. The knife was so sharp that I cut myself badly.

15. They never said that they would arrive late.

16. The old car crept slowly along the deeply rutted roads.

17. Suddenly he discovered that he could not walk.

18. The men felt tired after their strenuous exertions, and they walked slowly and silently to their homes.

19. He reads very fast, but he is poor at remembering what he has read.

20. In a very important decision, the Supreme Court unanimously outlawed segregation in public schools.

21. The lazy child finally got up and asked his mother for some breakfast.

22. The quality of gasoline is governed almost entirely by the various processes used in refining it.

23. The cake tasted so good that nearly all of it was eaten before Mother had even served herself.

24. The series of long and seemingly endless consultations was finally concluded.

25. The rhythm of Indian music is based on a pattern that is repeated over and over.

14 COMPARISON OF ADJECTIVES AND ADVERBS

Section 4E, *Essentials of English*

In the spaces provided, write the comparative and superlative degrees of the following adjectives and adverbs.

EXAMPLES:	*Comparative*	*Superlative*
nice	nicer	nicest
heavenly	more heavenly	most heavenly

1. pretty

2. miserable

3. quickly

4. little

5. ill

6. good

7. beautiful

8. quietly

9. dignified

10. serene

In each of the following sentences, the positive degree of an adjective or an adverb is placed in parentheses. Choose the form (comparative or superlative) which is required by the context, and write it in the space provided.

EXAMPLE:

He was the (noble) Roman of them all.   noblest

11. John was the (tall) of the twins.

12. He grew (rapidly) than his brother.

13. It was the (warm) day of the year.

14. Bananas are (hard) to digest than peaches.

15. Many clever plans were submitted, but mine was the (original).

16. Stupidity is bad, but dishonesty is (bad) than stupidity.

17. The soup was good, the main course was excellent, but (good) of all was the dessert.

18. Both father and son were self-possessed, but the father seemed to be the (dignified).

19. Frank was the (well) dressed student in the whole class.

20. I'll buy whichever of the two cars is (cheap).

21. Of the many ways of going to San Francisco, Father chose the one which would be (quick).

22. My parents are so broadminded that it is hard to say which is the (liberal).

23. Both of them dressed well, but Jane's clothes were (sensible).

24. He was the (rich) man in town.

25. The company advertised that its brand of soap was (cheap) than all the others.

15 CORRECT USE OF ADJECTIVES AND ADVERBS

Section 4F, *Essentials of English*

Each of the following sentences contains two modifiers in parentheses. Choose the modifier which is correct in the context of the sentence and write it in the space provided.

EXAMPLE:

She sang (sweet, sweetly).   sweetly

1. The water in the tub felt (hot, hotly).

2. The boy felt (hot, hotly) after the ball game.

3. John felt (bad, badly) about losing the game

4. The food looked and tasted (good, well) to the hungry men.

5. The carpenter built the house (good, well).

6. He was (real, really) sorry to retire from his position.

7. After the visit from the skunk, the house smelled pretty (bad, badly).

8. The children were (quiet, quietly) all afternoon.

9. They were playing (quiet, quietly) in the cellar.

10. The hunters were (sure, surely) glad to see the truck returning with more supplies.

11. This coat is (some, somewhat) warmer than the other one.

12. The army fought (fierce, fiercely) all afternoon.

13. The violinist was so tired that he was unable to play (good, well).

14. I don't like my coffee very (sweet, sweetly).

_____

15. He got to the meeting so (quick, quickly) that he had to wait for the others.

_____

16. James seemed (wonderful, wonderfully) rested after his vacation.

_____

17. He was able to cut the wood (easier, more easily) after he sharpened the axe.

_____

18. The car stopped so (sudden, suddenly) that the groceries fell off the seat.

_____

19. The runner found himself (easy, easily) in the lead after the first lap.

_____

20. The laboratory looked (horrible, horribly) after the experiments were finished.

_____

21. Whatever is worth doing at all is worth doing (good, well).

_____

22. The clerks were (terrible, terribly) afraid of their new boss.

_____

23. The band leading the parade sounded (good, well) to the marchers.

_____

24. He paid a (considerable, considerably) higher price than he was able to afford.

_____

25. The players looked (smart, smartly) in their new uniforms.

_____

16 IDENTIFYING VERBALS

Section 5, *Essentials of English*

A verbal is italicized in each of the following sentences. Indicate the particular form of the verbal (present or perfect infinitive, present or present perfect participle, past or past perfect participle) in the space provided at the right.

EXAMPLE:

Having learned his lesson, he closed the book.   present perfect participle
_____

1. I expect *to see* you soon.
_____

2. He was tired of *being* sick all the time.
_____

3. The operation *known* as "Pathfinder" was successful.
_____

4. *Bowling* is a pleasant and relaxing game.
_____

5. *To have completed* the assignment by Sunday is too much to hope for.
_____

6. *Having been chosen* for the part, she refused to accept it.
_____

7. It was a pleasure to see the child *eating* a hearty meal.
_____

8. Men seldom rebel against anything that doesn't deserve *rebelling* against.
_____

9. I expect *to be watching* the ball game all afternoon.
_____

10. Make the driver *stop* at the next corner.
_____

Each of the following sentences contains a participle. Identify the participle and write it in the first space to the right. If it is used as a noun, write *gerund* in the second space.

EXAMPLES:

He was tired of reading.	reading	gerund
Fearing a storm, the captain dropped anchor.	fearing	

11. Lending books is a good way to lose them. _____ _____

12. Any story told too often loses its point. _____ _____

13. It was hard to read in the fading light. _____ _____

14. Knowing where to find information about a subject is often as valuable as knowledge of the subject. _____ _____

15. There is no harm in reaching for a star. _____ _____

16. The child's screaming got on her nerves. _____ _____

17. The screaming child was sent to bed. _____ _____

18. Convinced that he was wrong, he finally apologized. _____ _____

19. The enemy showed courage and daring. _____ _____

20. He hates meeting new people. _____ _____

21. Having slept all morning, he had breakfast at noon. _____ _____

22. Real knowledge is knowing what you know and what you don't know. _____ _____

23. They wrote their names on the newly whitewashed walls. _____ _____

24. He liked to talk, but he was better at listening. _____ _____

25. I couldn't help laughing when I saw what had happened. _____ _____

17 POSSESSIVES BEFORE GERUNDS

Sections 5B and 1D, *Essentials of English*

Each of the following sentences contains a participle. Some of these participles function as adjectives; others are gerunds. When a gerund appears in any of the following sentences, the noun preceding it should be placed in the possessive case. Make such changes as are necessary by writing the correct possessive form of the noun in the space to the right.

EXAMPLE:

Mary, wearing a party dress, was beautiful to behold.

Mary wearing a party dress was an unusual event.   Mary's

1. Everybody admired John swimming because it was an ability he had acquired with great effort.

2. Everybody admired John swimming because of his magnificent physique.

3. Mr. Jones, seizing every opportunity that came his way, rapidly climbed the ladder of success.

4. We were irritated at the racket caused by the boys shouting, but we were pleased by its indication that they were enjoying themselves.

5. The peach sitting on the window sill is probably ripe.

6. The firm deciding to go out of business came as a surprise to the employees.

7. We were very much pleased by the class agreeing to give such an appropriate gift to the school.

8. Mary getting married was an event which delighted all her friends.

9. Johnson being made a star in the play was an honor he richly deserved.

10. Johnson, being made a star in the play, became too arrogant to bear.

11. We bought an old record so we could listen to Caruso singing which we so much admired.

12. Frank winning the contest was more than we dared hope for.

13. Frank, winning the contest, said that nobody could be more surprised than he was.

_____

14. Mother cooking was always something to look forward to.

_____

15. It was a pleasure to watch Mary doing her homework because her face always assumed an almost dedicated expression.

_____

16. The men smoking bothered my mother because she hated the smell.

_____

17. We wanted to watch the women weaving exhibit.

_____

18. Fred was so hungry that he couldn't keep his eyes off the fish frying in the pan.

_____

19. The jury voted for his acquittal because the chief witness lying was obvious to all of them.

_____

20. Ned knot-tying was a skill he had acquired in the Navy.

_____

21. The children, digging in the sand all afternoon, were hot and tired.

_____

22. The children digging in the sand resulted in many strange shapes and contours on the beach.

_____

23. Henry Aaron hitting 715 home runs was one of the greatest ball players of all time.

_____

24. Babe Ruth hitting 714 home runs made him second only to Henry Aaron.

_____

25. Thurgood Marshall becoming the first black Supreme Court justice pleased many Americans.

_____

18 IDENTIFYING CONJUNCTIONS AND PREPOSITIONS

Section 6, *Essentials of English*

The italicized word in each of the following sentences is either a preposition or a conjunction. Indicate which it is by writing *prep.* (preposition) or *conj.* (conjunction) in the first space to the right. If it is a preposition, write its object in the second space.

EXAMPLES:

Nobody was there *but* Henry.   prep.   Henry

I tried *but* I couldn't do it.   conj.

1. Nobody has emptied the garbage *since* yesterday.

2. We have been unhappy *since* you went away.

3. The summer days were very warm, *but* the nights were cool and pleasant.

4. She never wore a hat, *for* she was very vain about her hair.

5. He did exactly *as* he was told.

6. There was nobody *like* him in the navy.

7. Repeat the sentence *after* me.

8. He came to the meeting *after* I left.

9. You know that as well *as* I.

10. Take the stale bread back *to* the store.

Each of the following sentences contains one conjunction and one preposition. Write the preposition in the first space to the right and the conjunction in the second space.

EXAMPLE: *Preposition*   *Conjunction*

Since you are leaving, we'll drive you to town.   to   since

11. Men, women, and children reached for life-preservers.

12. They walked around the block because they wanted the exercise.

13. When I got home for supper, the house was deserted.

14. Baking is difficult unless you have a good oven in your kitchen.

15. Sing some songs with me while I wash the dishes.

16. Laurel and Hardy are very funny in their films.

17. There was plenty of food although it was hard to find anything appetizing.

18. Go into the house whenever you are ready.

19. The thunder was followed by such a heavy rain that it soaked us thoroughly.

20. It has been estimated that about 19% of Americans live in integrated communities.

21. I shall try to get home before morning if I possibly can.

22. Let me begin by saying that I am very pleased to be here.

23. Few men about town dress more smartly than he.

24. A sound like distant gunfire or bombing broke the silence.

25. Put a shawl around your shoulders before you go out.

19 REVIEW: IDENTIFYING THE PARTS OF SPEECH

Sections 1-8, *Essentials of English*

Write the conventional dictionary abbreviation of the part of speech of each italicized word in the following selection.

In the eighteenth *century*, as American Indian children grew older, they *became* increasingly conscious of the roles they would one day be assuming as men and women. Little boys *in* the Creek Nation learned early to *eschew* a woman's work, and they were careful to avoid even a suggestion of the tasks that occupied *little* girls: maintaining the fires, helping with the making of baskets and *pots*, gardening, and housework. *Instead,* Creek boys began at an early age to learn the skills of the hunter by roving *through* the forests, shooting at small game or targets with their scaled-down bows and arrows. *Strongly* ingrained in them was the *importance* of the stoical virtue of withstanding pain *without* crying out. They would have contests to see which of them could silently *endure* the most stings by wasps and yellow jackets. The boys were taught when very young that *their* advancement in the Nation depended on their success as warriors. *Other* abilities, such as *oratory*, giving wise counsel, and being stoical in times of trial, were *honored* by the Creek nation, but no ability was so honored as that exemplified by the warrior brave. The boys knew *that* there would come a day *when* they must prove themselves as warriors by bringing in a *scalp*. Only then would they gain a council seat, in the public square. *Until* that day of honor, they would remain in a kind of disgrace, being given the *menial* tasks of lighting the warrior's pipes, hauling wood for the *ceremonial* fires, and cooking the black drink for the *braves*.

Cooking the black drink was not a *meaningless* task for the young Creeks, *however;* it placed them near the seats of power in the council

	n.
	v.i.
	prep.
1.	
2.	
3.	
4.	
5.	
6.	
7.	
8.	
9.	
10.	
11.	
12.	
13.	
14.	
15.	
16.	
17.	
18.	
19.	
20.	
21.	
22.	

of chiefs, enabling them to *overhear* the verbal flourishes, the ora- 23. _____

tory, and the debate. The black drink *was brewed*, as William Bartram 24. _____

observed, in an open shed *directly* opposite the door of the town house 25. _____

where the council meeting was held. This dark-brewed ritual beverage, 26. _____

made from *holly* leaves, held a central place in the life of the Creeks, 27. _____

and they believed that it purified the body by acting as an *emetic*, 28. _____

causing them to *expel* the contents of their stomachs by vomiting. 29. _____

LeClerc Milfort, who was introduced to this spectacle almost *immediately* 30. _____

upon his *arrival* in the Creek Nation, thought it sickening and disgusting 31. _____

to see the braves *retching* in the council meetings, sometimes 32. _____

holding their arms across their chests in a ceremonial manner and pro- 33. _____

jecting their vomit six or eight feet. He had an interesting *theory*, 34. _____

however, *concerning* the practical reason for this ritual, which, he 35. _____

wrote, "appears only ridiculous at first, [but] has *nonetheless* a very 36. _____

wise basis, and which would not always be *out of* place in the assem- 37. _____

blies of civilized peoples." The purpose, as Milfort *understood* it, 38. _____

was to assure the *chief* of the assembly that each member had a stomach 39. _____

free of food and strong liquors and therefore had a clear head for the 40. _____

council *deliberations*. 41. _____

20 IDENTIFYING SUBJECTS

Section 9A, *Essentials of English*

In the following sentences place the complete subject in parentheses and write the simple or compound subject in the space to the right.

EXAMPLE:

(Our country) now has fifty states.   country

1. My neighbor loves New Orleans jazz.

2. My neighbor on the right loves Viennese waltzes.

3. Rent is a large item in our budget.

4. Rent and food are the largest items in our budget.

5. Every morning before breakfast he takes a long walk.

6. Is there any reason for apologizing to him?

7. The schedule of trains on the West Suburban Transit Line has been reduced forty per cent.

8. Fold the paper on the dotted line and tear it straight across.

9. How long does the journey from New York to San Francisco take by jet airplane?

10. Modern city planners must be particularly aware of the need for adequate mass transportation.

11. Richard Wright's famous novel *Native Son* was published in 1940.

12. The vacant lot used by children playing cowboys and Indians was recently given to the city for a park.

13. After all the rain this summer, the weeds have completely taken over my vegetable garden.

14. Mine is the red hat.

_____

15. Basketball and handball are his favorite sports.

_____

16. His favorite sports are basketball and handball.

_____

17. There were twenty-seven different kinds of pie on sale at the fair last year.

_____

18. Seldom was food so rapidly consumed.

_____

19. Neither John nor Jerry is eligible for the team.

_____

20. The children in the lower grades were led through the side exit into the play yard.

_____

21 IDENTIFYING PREDICATES

Section 9B, *Essentials of English*

In the following sentences place the complete predicate in parentheses and write the simple or compound predicate in the space to the right.

EXAMPLE:

The shop in Windsor(contained a wide variety of wares)   contained

1. Plastic toys break easily.

2. We put our hopes in the United Nations.

3. The mechanic checked the points and spark plugs and adjusted the carburetor.

4. During the crisis, we spent much of our time reading the papers and listening to the news.

5. Praise the Lord and pass the ammunition.

6. Are the subways running on time this morning?

7. By next October he will have been serving as town clerk for thirty-two years.

8. After all those years, he finally married his childhood sweetheart, the girl next door.

9. Very often the slaves tried to run away, but generally without success.

10. Despite their apparent recklessness, his actions were always governed by his innate caution.

11. To become a successful business man much else besides capital is necessary.

12. Capture by the Indians was the most dreaded fate of all.

13. After years of failures and miscalculations, Carruthers had finally perfected his formula.

14. Lesson by lesson, exercise by exercise he plodded through the manual.

15. On the corner near the subway exit sat the old man on the curb.

16. He was summoned before the grand jury and questioned about his connection with the Homex Building Corporation.

17. There in the sand beneath the end of the dock lay the ring.

18. The program lists the names of all the contributors, no matter how small their donations.

19. His diaries betray his inner contradictions and show a man filled with doubt.

20. For the first ten years of his marriage he was a devoted husband and father.

22 IDENTIFYING PHRASES

Section 9C, *Essentials of English*

Put parentheses around the phrases in the following sentences. In the space to the right identify each phrase as prepositional (prep.), infinitive (inf.), gerund (gerund), participial (part.), or as a verb phrase.

EXAMPLE:

The apple tree is (in full bloom.)

prep.

1. A boy of sixteen guided us.

2. Trembling with rage, he stalked out. _____

3. He dove from the high board. _____

4. Everyone has been awaiting you impatiently. _____

5. To be accepted is what every child desires. _____

6. Collecting stamps is an interesting hobby. _____

7. Stop at the first filling station. _____

8. We may be victorious yet. _____

9. Many technical writers work for the Atomex Research Association. _____

10. A scientist likes to experiment. _____

11. She enjoys reading novels. _____

12. I have been singing his praises. _____

13. The man talking to Mother is the new teacher. _____

14. His first task, learning the English language, took him three months. ⎯⎯⎯⎯⎯

15. The publication of *The Communist Manifesto* precipitated a crisis. ⎯⎯⎯⎯⎯

16. The most popular novelist of the year is not always the winner of the Pulitzer Prize. ⎯⎯⎯⎯⎯

17. The deer halted for a moment. ⎯⎯⎯⎯⎯

18. Stained a red-brown, this wood looks handsome. ⎯⎯⎯⎯⎯

19. Proud of his achievements, civilized man scorns his more primitive brothers. ⎯⎯⎯⎯⎯

20. The existing races required ages to develop. ⎯⎯⎯⎯⎯

21. I shall be happy when I see the manuscript. ⎯⎯⎯⎯⎯

22. The father took his son for a long walk. ⎯⎯⎯⎯⎯

23. They went into the woods while it was still light. ⎯⎯⎯⎯⎯

24. Having no money, he accepted whatever people gave him. ⎯⎯⎯⎯⎯

25. A wise person banks some of his salary every month. ⎯⎯⎯⎯⎯

23 IDENTIFYING INDEPENDENT CLAUSES

Section 9C, *Essentials of English*

In the following sentences identify the independent clauses by enclosing them in parentheses.

EXAMPLE:

(He invested the money)that he earned.

1. He is the man who spoke to me.

2. The director scolded, and the actors sulked.

3. During the seventeenth century, many actors achieved great fame, but they were not considered respectable members of society.

4. When you plan a garden, you must take into account the annual temperature range in your area.

5. Everyone knows that man's rate of development is abnormally slow in comparison to that of other animals.

6. Eugenics is not a branch of natural science; it is a branch of social science.

7. Many animals can show that they are hungry, but only man can ask for bread or an egg.

8. Since evolution has a large number of blind alleys, it is like a maze with many wrong turnings.

9. The scientific method refuses to ask questions that cannot be answered.

10. Although he was not a member of the association, he attended many of its meetings.

11. Because the city is reorganizing its housing agencies, the City Manager has not yet selected the agency to handle the loan fund.

12. They felt that a sidewalk café would not be self-supporting.

13. The silver dollar is favored on the West Coast, but few of them appear elsewhere.

14. Because they feared the effects of a strike on helpless patients, hospitals long refused to accept unions and collective bargaining.

15. Mozart, who was a musical genius and a child prodigy, died young.

16. It has been said, and the point appears in this article, that the need for worker priests is due to the shortage of ordination candidates caused by the war.

17. Using his concept of the devil as a stick for beating everything he disapproves of in the modern world, he shows himself to be a reactionary in the most formal sense of the term.

18. Where there is marriage without love, there will be love without marriage.

19. Who is so deaf as he who will not hear?

20. He thinks that a liberal is a bad man who is full of evil motives.

21. When evening comes, the townspeople pull the shutters down over their shop windows and return to their homes.

22. We hoped that our guests would not arrive until we had completed our preparations for dinner.

23. If everybody did exactly as he pleased at all times, there would be more trouble in the world than there is now.

24. Jonathan Edwards, who was an outstanding Puritan preacher, was an intellectual who devoted most of his great mental ability to the analysis and attempted solution of religious problems.

25. He did not try to avoid issues which were unpopular or difficult to cope with.

24 IDENTIFYING DEPENDENT CLAUSES

Section 9C, *Essentials of English*

In the following sentences identify the dependent clauses by enclosing them in parentheses. In the space to the right tell whether the clause is used as a noun, an adjective, or an adverb.

EXAMPLE:

This is the provision(that he objects to.)   adjective

1. They hoped that the war would end soon.

2. Franklin Delano Roosevelt died before he had completed his last term of office.

3. Peter was the disciple who denied Jesus three times.

4. Do you agree that an unexamined life is not worth living?

5. Matthew Herson, who was an Afro-American member of Perry's expedition, placed the American flag at the North Pole.

6. Because man's aggressiveness can be canalized into other outlets, war is not inevitable for him.

7. We must find what William James called "a moral equivalent for war".

8. As H. G. Wells said, warfare may yet turn back the clock of civilization and throw the world into another dark age.

9. Annsville, Maine, is a little community which is entirely dependent on timber.

10. He reminded us that Darwin has been called the Newton of biology.

11. Once the brain reaches a certain complexity, it controls human behavior.

12. In *Common Sense about the War* Shaw insisted that the war must be supported.

13. The Department of Labor estimated that a third of American married women were gainfully employed.

14. The American Telephone and Telegraph Company reported that the number of its employees reached one million for the first time in 1979.

   _____

15. The NAACP, which was founded in 1910, accomplished a great deal in the struggle for civil rights.

   _____

16. We must strike while the iron is hot.

   _____

17. If wishes were horses, beggars would ride.

   _____

18. Because he often secured agreement, or the appearance of it, the Ambassador's diplomatic powers tended to be overrated.

   _____

19. Although the election appeared to be lost, he campaigned as vigorously as ever.

   _____

20. He who dances must pay the piper.

   _____

25 RECOGNIZING TYPES OF SENTENCES

Section 9D, *Essentials of English*

In the space to the right of each sentence state whether the sentence is simple, complex, compound, or compound-complex.

EXAMPLE:

The president is the chief executive. _____simple_____

1. Facts are stubborn things. _____

2. The veracity which increases with old age is not far from folly. _____

3. His last novel, which I shall discuss later, raises serious questions about the origins of his inspiration. _____

4. They never went more than a hundred miles from the city, nor were they ever away for more than a month. _____

5. It must be admitted that his letters are dull. _____

6. The most interesting of his gifts to the museum was a large collection of gowns. _____

7. The brothers opened an office in Detroit, but soon after, as we have seen, Dr. Nils abandoned it to become a medical missionary in Liberia. _____

8. In those days it was a father's duty not to spare the rod. _____

9. It is better to have loved and lost than never to have loved at all. _____

10. It has been demonstrated that an insufficiency of vitamins results in retardation of growth. _____

11. In ancient Egypt there was much need of surgery; this fact is shown by archeological surveys. _____

12. Kings were once thought to have the miraculous ability to cure by the laying on of hands. _____

13. We always love those who admire us, but we do not always love those whom we admire.

_____

14. In June 1982 the Equal Rights Amendment was not approved by enough states to make it a part of the United States Constitution.

_____

15. In his religious writings he gave the age what it was ready to receive.

_____

16. Like Descartes, Locke regards our own existence as the first of all certainties.

_____

17. I have been to Disneyland five times, and I am still alive.

_____

18. A maternity welfare station had been established in her community, but she refused to visit it.

_____

19. She had been taught enough German to recite three of Heine's short lyrics.

_____

20. He believes that might makes right.

_____

21. His was a voice that was crying in the wilderness.

_____

22. A peptic ulcer is a small wound which develops either in the stomach or the duodenum.

_____

23. In this apparatus, if the rat jumps at the right window, it obtains food; if it jumps at the wrong window, it does not open, and the rat falls to the floor.

_____

24. In personality the changes are often marked.

_____

25. Some Bedouins discovered the Dead Sea Scrolls in a well-concealed cave.

_____

26 RECOGNIZING SENTENCE FRAGMENTS

Section 10, *Essentials of English*

In the space to the right state whether each of the following expressions is a sentence or a sentence fragment.

EXAMPLE:

When the capital moved to Leningrad.   fragment

1. While he was serving his residency at Eastern General Hospital.

2. He refused.

3. To be a member of an archeological expedition to Guatemala.

4. Who discovered insulin for the control of diabetes.

5. Who discovered insulin for the control of diabetes?

6. A conflict of interests which smoldered for decades and blazed into the Civil War.

7. Inasmuch as his experience on the bench has been limited to magistrates courts.

8. Because corporations which spend thousands of dollars for computers want large and showy machines.

9. An engineering feat marred by the fact that eighteen construction men lost their lives.

10. It requires total dedication to become a biochemist.

11. Even before Henry Hudson sailed the *Half Moon* up the river in search of a northwest passage.

12. As long as the government continues to subsidize farmers for limiting certain crops.

13. The Harding administration was full of corruption.

14. Today the compact automobile is popular.

_____

15. As painful as it is to be a non-conformist in an age of conformity.

_____

16. His statement that absolute power corrupts absolutely.

_____

17. That commuter railroads are being bankrupted by the automobile.

_____

18. Since the time when the Wright brothers flew their first airplane.

_____

19. The term *muckraker* was first used by Theodore Roosevelt.

_____

20. While millions of people all over the world are dying of starvation.

_____

21. Believing, as I do, that men do not live by bread alone.

_____

22. You cannot make bricks without straw.

_____

23. And was finally killed by Al Capone's gang in the St. Valentine's Day Massacre.

_____

24. The Auxiliary is running a raffle in order to purchase beds for the new wing of the hospital.

_____

25. A moody, irascible man who hates animals and children.

_____

27 IDENTIFYING AND CORRECTING SENTENCE FRAGMENTS

Section 10, *Essentials of English*

In the space to the right state whether each of the following expressions is a sentence or a sentence fragment. Change the sentence fragments to sentences by removing the subordinating word with parentheses and by capitalizing the first word wherever necessary.

EXAMPLES:

We filled many evenings by playing charades and cards.   sentence

(While) the orchestra was playing the overture.   fragment

1. That we should be allowed to travel freely abroad. _____

2. Franklin Delano Roosevelt who was elected president for four terms. _____

3. When the Bowery was a shady lane extending from the Battery to Peter Stuyvesant's farm. _____

4. The understudy was standing in the wings, ready to go on at a moment's notice. _____

5. Because management has obstinately refused to negotiate with the union. _____

6. We have examined thoroughly the qualifications of the surgeons on the panel. _____

7. Since the Volstead Act was repealed. _____

8. Although many influential Americans supported the Spanish Loyalists. _____

9. Because Prime Minister Chamberlain desired peace in our time. _____

10. The Maginot Line crumbled before the German onslaught. _____

11. A large elm that was shattered by lightning. _____

12. Provided that the Bar Association endorses his candidacy. _____

13. When the Japanese attacked Pearl Harbor.

        _____

14. The ground is blanketed with snow from November to April.

        _____

15. The second communiqué that was issued on February 6 of that year.

        _____

16. Several mechanical defects of the heart that can now be corrected by surgery.

        _____

17. In this area where the land is too rocky for cultivation.

        _____

18. And the tomato which was then called a love apple and was considered poisonous.

        _____

19. When the Soviet Union launched the first earth satellite.

        _____

20. The problem of the Wetbacks in California has not yet been solved.

        _____

21. Where is my watch?

        _____

22. Where my cat sleeps every night on her blanket.

        _____

23. Abraham Lincoln who believed that freeing the slaves would end the war sooner.

        _____

24. As time goes by.

        _____

25. A butterfly's wings which are really too large for efficient flying.

        _____

28 IDENTIFYING AND COMPLETING SENTENCE FRAGMENTS

Section 10, *Essentials of English*

In the space to the right state whether the following expressions are sentences or sentence fragments. Complete the fragments by changing the verbals to finite verbs and adding a subject and predicate if necessary.

EXAMPLE:

Stamp collecting being an interesting and profitable hobby.   fragment
_____

Stamp collecting is an . . .

_____

1. The delegate from India discussing the issue before the General Assembly of the United Nations.   _____

_____

2. To pitch the only no-hit no-run game of the season.   _____

_____

3. Carried on their shoulders by his teammates, he was thrilled beyond words.   _____

_____

4. The National Urban League which was founded in 1911.   _____

_____

5. An outstanding poet, Robert Frost.   _____

_____

6. In 1949, the war being over, but not the unrest.   _____

_____

7. The clay jars still containing some fragments of manuscripts made of papyrus.

_____

_____

8. After Solomon's death the Kingdom was divided into two countries,

_____

_____

9. Their white robes and cowls covering them from head to foot.

_____

_____

10. Telling his benefactor that he had been appointed lecturer in the University of Padua.

_____

_____

29 IDENTIFYING AND COMPLETING SENTENCE FRAGMENTS

Section 10, *Essentials of English*

In the space to the right state whether each of the following expressions is a sentence fragment or a sentence. In the space below complete the sentence fragment by writing an independent clause to which the fragment is properly related.

EXAMPLE:

When the mob began to gather.   fragment
. . . martial law was declared.

_____

1. And has been knocked out in the third round by the superannuated Tornado Barnes.   _____

_____

2. While he was clerking for Jenkins and Company, he was also studying law.   _____

_____

3. Although it has been proved that there is some connection between cancer of the throat and smoking.   _____

_____

4. While he was stationed in Paris after the war.   _____

_____

5. Females numbering well over 50 percent of the population.   _____

_____

6. How to insure the peace was the people's only concern.   _____

_____

7. A stern disciplinarian is what the class needs.

      _____

_____

8. The fastest and most exciting of sports.

      _____

_____

9. As long as I am charged with enforcing the law.

      _____

_____

10. More than 25 percent of all black families are headed by a woman.

      _____

_____

30 DETECTING COMMA FAULTS

Section 11, *Essentials of English*

Some of the sentences below are correct; some contain a comma fault. If the sentence is correct, write "C" in the space to the right. If the sentence is incorrect, circle the comma fault and write "CF" in the space to the right.

EXAMPLE:

My son would be my only assistant, I had good reason for wanting no one else. **CF**

1. A sudden gust of wind blew out the candle, we had to grope our way through the cellar. _____

2. The chairman has an engagement, the meeting will have to be postponed. _____

3. He will not seek the nomination, nor will he accept a draft. _____

4. The cello played a rocking bass, and the violin embroidered a soaring melody above it. _____

5. He says that he is sixty-eight, however, the records show that he is seventy-three. _____

6. The camp is small and lacking in facilities, but the site is beautiful, and the staff is efficient. _____

7. None of the other guests could be late for meals, this was a privilege granted Frau Gantner alone. _____

8. Human behavior is complicated, consequently, we identify human elements with the most complicated areas of the brain. _____

9. Severe pain shocks office workers and others who seldom experience injuries, whereas construction workers take their injuries in stride. _____

10. When both parents are diabetic, their children will probably become diabetic. _____

11. The wood was not allowed to season properly, consequently, the doors of the cabinet have warped. _____

12. The revolutionary tide was stemmed, and the Holy Alliance kept revolt at bay. _____

13. The Valley Brook school has been condemned, nevertheless, the Board of Education continues to use it as an annex for vocational classes. _____

14. The new box is large and attractively designed, perhaps it will stimulate the sale of Britex. _____

15. All leading stocks have declined in price for the third consecutive day, yet trading remains brisk and optimistic. _____

16. The land has been cleared and graded and the foundation poured, undoubtedly the house will be ready for occupancy by September 1. _____

17. The quotation is, "Nothing emboldens sin so much as mercy," did Shakespeare write it? _____

18. Ray Robinson was an outstanding boxer, he was the first to win the Edward J. Neil Memorial Plaque. _____

19. Sea-faring men range over the earth, but the external objects they have encountered can form no consistent picture upon their imagination. _____

20. If the perfect historian should write the history of America, he would assuredly not omit the contributions of minority groups. _____

21. A mood of melancholy tension is the great American problem, not inflation, nor the rackets, nor farm subsidies. _____

22. The magazine is now concerned with the candidates for the comptroller's office, it sent a representative to interview them. _____

23. There are two ways of understanding nature, we can understand it as a machine and as a work. _____

24. A narrow mind is thought to contain little knowledge; an enlarged one, to contain a great deal. _____

25. Penguins are amusing and interesting birds, their natural habitat is the Antarctic. _____

31 PUNCTUATING INDEPENDENT CLAUSES

Sections 11 and 12, *Essentials of English*

Each of the following sentences contains two independent clauses which should be separated by a comma or a semi-colon. Insert the proper mark of punctuation as follows:

There are few mosquitoes here‸I haven't been bitten this summer.

1. He is an electronic engineer he designs and builds computers.

2. He has not paid his bill for over a year consequently we must cancel his membership.

3. The captain gave three sharp blasts on the whistle and the boat began to slip away from the pier.

4. Their relationship was stormy but the marriage was not devoid of love and respect.

5. Generally, a man is not taxed in two states he pays his tax either where he resides or where he works.

6. Every responsible citizen is aware of the need for a new school yet the bond issue has been defeated for three consecutive years.

7. He failed as a salesman for his temperament was singularly un-commercial.

8. The most dreadful fate of all was capture by the Indians and this was not infrequent.

9. He sought expert advice before purchasing a picture neverthless, he was frequently duped.

10. Either the bill is paid by the first of the month or the furniture will be repossessed.

11. The counsel was unable to appear therefore the inquiry was adjourned until a later date.

12. The more austere priests were opposed to pilgrimages they pointed out that there were easier ways to gain God's pardon.

13. Among the local men's shops, the Bon Ton, owned by Murray Harris, was the most popular it offered the largest selection at the lowest prices in town.

14. The wine made in this valley is excellent it is as good as any made in France.

15. He did not dare to leave his business in Salt Lake City but he instructed his partner to buy the parcels of land along the waterfront.

16. One was murdered by a native the other four escaped on a raft.

17. For centuries men have tried to reduce the written word to its simplest form and their efforts have produced a vast literature on systems of shorthand.

18. Mr. Donley's book about printing for the trade is generally excellent yet he omits two or three important authorities.

19. Repression may be harmful however, it is necessary for dealing with conflict in early life before rational judgment has developed.

20. Words are tools they carve concepts out of experience.

21. The New York Knickerbockers were all great players but their success was owed in part to the scoring ability of Willis Reed.

22. Hyperbole, the last figure of speech we shall discuss, is gross exaggeration it overstates, but does not intend to deceive.

23. Halley's comet is the largest known comet it cuts an elliptical course through the solar system.

24. Halley observed the comet in 1682 and it was named for him.

25. The head and tail of the comet are not incandescent and they are not burning up through friction.

32 LOCATING DIVISION POINTS BETWEEN SENTENCES

Sections 11 and 12, *Essentials of English*

The following has been printed without any terminal marks of punctuation. Place an X at the end of each sentence. Write the first word of each sentence, properly capitalized, in the space to the right, directly opposite the line in which it occurs. The first sentence is correctly indicated, as are the ends of paragraphs.

1. The trend of higher education in the United States has

2. changed significantly since the last century X the aim of — **The**

3. college used to be the production of a well-read gentle-

4. man education for women was almost unknown Jane Austen in

5. the early nineteenth century remarked that a woman who knew

6. anything should conceal it as well as she could.

7. Now there are women's colleges, coed colleges, and col-

8. leges for nearly anyone in addition to colleges which grant

9. degrees for the humanities and sciences, there are many vo-

10. cational and technical training courses beyond the high school

11. level it has been estimated that two million American stu-

12. dents are now taking advantage of advanced training some of

13. these are in four-year technical institutions most of them

14. are enrolled in two-year junior or community colleges the

15. most obvious advantage of the community college is its low-

16. er cost tuition is free in many publicly supported insti-

17. tutions, and the college is within commuting distance many

18. of them hold evening classes, making it possible for stu-

19. dents to support themselves by full-time or part-time em-

20. ployment a number of business firms will even pay part or

21. all of the tuition of their employees the demand for grad-

22. uates of vocational colleges is so great in some parts of _____

23. the country that industries seek out students and offer _____

24. them positions before their graduation. _____

25.   At most community colleges, there is an open admission _____

26. policy this means that any high school graduate may enter _____

27. without taking entrance examinations some two-year colleges _____

28. will even enroll students who do not have a high school _____

29. diploma. _____

30.   The number of junior colleges has almost doubled in the _____

31. last ten years there are now more than a thousand of them _____

32. in America in most of them students may choose an entire- _____

33. ly academic curriculum, enabling them to transfer to a _____

34. four-year college if their records are good if they are _____

35. interested only in vocational training, they may graduate _____

36. with an appropriate degree many academic courses are open _____

37. to both kinds of students of those who have transferred _____

38. to a senior college, nearly all have been successful an _____

39. important difference between junior and senior colleges is _____

40. that a two-year college is apt to place emphasis on its _____

41. faculty's teaching ability most four-year colleges are like- _____

42. ly to be more interested in scholarly attainments there is _____

43. no doubt that the two-year colleges have made possible ed- _____

44. ucational opportunities for thousands who would have been _____

45. denied the chance of higher education without them. _____

33 LOCATING DIVISION POINTS BETWEEN SENTENCES

Sections 11 and 12, *Essentials of English*

The following has been printed without any terminal marks of punctuation. Place an X at the end of each sentence. Write the first word of each sentence, properly capitalized, in the space to the right, directly opposite the line in which it occurs. The first sentence is correctly indicated, as are the ends of paragraphs.

1. For Mark Twain, the June voyage on the S.S. *Minneapolis*

2. was one of the most exciting events of his life **X** in May   In

0. the newspapers throughout the country had announced that

4. Twain had been invited to England to receive an honorary

5. degree from Oxford University—the first humorist to be so

6. honored when he received the cable announcement, he commented:

7. "I never expected to cross the water again, but I would

8. be willing to journey to Mars for that Oxford degree."

9. He sailed on June 8, which was, by a curious coincidence,

10. exactly 40 years from the day he had sailed on the *Quaker*

11. *City* for Europe it was that first voyage that provided

12. material for *Innocents Abroad* and contributed to his early

13. fame his friend and biographer, Albert Bigelow Paine, went

14. to the ship to bid him good-bye to Paine, Mark "seemed a

15. little sad, remembering, I think, the wife, who would have

16. enjoyed this honor with him, but could not share it now."

17. His wife, Olivia, had died in 1904 her death was the

18. latest in a chain of events that had saddened this man

19. who had spent most of his life making the world laugh

20. those aboard the S.S. *Minneapolis* saw a man who had lived

21. through many disasters: his publishing firm had failed; he

22. had lost his fortune as well as his wife's by backing

23. an unsuccessful new type-setting machine; his oldest daughter,

24. Susan, died, and his youngest daughter had developed

25. epilepsy.

26.   But the voyage on the well-appointed and spacious *Min-*

27. *neapolis* seems to have been a pleasant one for Twain Albert

28. B. Paine attributes much of the pleasantness of the

29. trip to the good company of Twain's fellow voyagers, in-

30. cluding "some very attractive young people—schoolgirls in

31. particular, such as all through life had appealed to Mark

32. Twain."

33.   Paine observed that young ladies, in Twain's later life,

34. "made a stronger appeal than ever the years had robbed

35. him of his own little flock, and always he was trying to

36. replace them" as Twain expressed it, "I had reached the

37. grandfather stage of life without grandchildren, so I began

38. to adopt some" Paine wrote that Twain "adopted several on

39. that journey to England."

34 RECOGNIZING FUSED SENTENCES

Section 12, *Essentials of English*

Some of the following sentences are fused and some are correct. In the space to the right write *correct* opposite each correct sentence. Mark the fused sentences *fused* and place an "X" at the point of fusion.

EXAMPLE:

Most shops were poor for a very simple reason✗their proprietors were also poor.   fused

1. With a mighty blow I struck my opponent fell to the ground.   _____

2. There is no denying that on his trip abroad the Ambassador talked foolishly he was an international joke.   _____

3. Senator Capriman spoke to the people over a national radio network as he announced he would.   _____

4. The magazine sells for seventy-five cents in Canada it costs eighty cents.   _____

5. The passengers were frightened by clouds of acrid smoke rolling through the coach.   _____

6. The singer included several unannounced songs in the morning he had changed the program.   _____

7. Laden with gifts for everyone, he came every Christmas eve he was the very embodiment of St. Nicholas.   _____

8. They taught the parakeet how to speak its words were hardly distinguishable.   _____

9. Lakefront property is very expensive for many people its cost is prohibitive.   _____

10. Make a careful search for the book there are several places in the attic where it might be.   _____

11. Fascism is resurgent in Germany despite the efforts of some eminent men to stamp it out.   _____

12. Small foreign cars are responsible for the popularity of the compact car in the United States.   _____

13. John Jacob Niles is an excellent folk singer he is also a collector and composer of songs.

14. Excursion boats make three trips a day from Memorial Day to Independence Day the round trip fare is $1.50.

15. We went crabbing every August in the shallow water of the creek we "scapped" soft shell crabs.

16. Concert pianists must practice constantly six or eight hours a day is not an unusual amount of time.

17. Group medicine and socialized medicine are frequently confused in the United States where many doctors are vehemently opposed to anything but private practice.

18. Veterans who have been on active duty for more than 80 days are entitled to receive monthly payments from the government for continuing their education.

19. "Hot dogs" are a typical American food even Mrs. Franklin Delano Roosevelt served them in the White House.

20. Mark Twain is the pseudonym for Samuel Clemens, the American humorist who wrote *Tom Sawyer*.

21. Aunt Belle went to the Yukon with her first husband when she was an old lady, she regaled us with stories about her adventures.

22. The Fabian Socialists advocated gradualism they believed in evolution, not revolution.

23. John Hunter was a pioneer in surgery his wife Anne wrote poems that were set to music by Haydn.

24. He had a job that I had never before heard of he was a jellybean polisher.

25. Jehol is a province in China that was incorporated into Manchukuo by the Japanese in 1935.

35 REVIEW: SENTENCE FRAGMENT, FUSED SENTENCE, AND COMMA FAULT

Sections 10, 11, 12, *Essentials of English*

Some of the expressions below are correct; others are incorrect. Analyze each expression and label it as follows in the space to the right:

C for a sentence

Frag. for a sentence fragment

CF for a comma fault. Circle the comma fault.

Fused for a fused sentence. Circle the point of fusion.

EXAMPLES:

The fringed gentian is a rare wild flower.	C
If the amendment is adopted.	Frag.
The bill passed both houses the President signed it.	CF
Nylon is a synthetic silk is a natural fiber.	Fused

1. The Bacchanalia was a Roman festival in honor of Bacchus. _____

2. Since the only photographic print was spoiled by fog. _____

3. Picasso was born in Spain, his early paintings were done in Paris. _____

4. The stump was handy he used it as a fulcrum. _____

5. The youth Ganymede being carried off by an eagle. _____

6. Use a lot of spice it will conceal the gamy flavor. _____

7. Somebody pried the cleats off the gangplank. _____

8. Galvani was an Italian physicist, he discovered that electricity may result from chemical action. _____

9. The gavotte is an old French dance. _____

10. This gear will not work it is stripped. _____

11. The term *hostler* is seldom used, it is archaic. _____

12. This cloth is spotlessly clean, it is immaculate. _____

13. Jet propulsion being a method of exerting force by means of a high-velocity jet discharged at the rear of an air or water craft. _____

14. Jubal, the son of Lamech, who purportedly invented musical instruments. _____

15. The purple berries of juniper are used for making gin. _____

16. The kangaroo is a marsupial, it is native to Australia. _____

17. The Klondike is a river it flows into the Yukon. _____

18. When he was a boy scout, he learned to tie many kinds of knots. _____

19. And also lacrosse which is a game of Indian origin. _____

20. To protect the chest with a heavy coat of lacquer. _____

21. Before coming to America he was a fisherman in the Lofoten Islands. _____

22. This plant is called love-in-a-mist, it is a most romantic name. _____

23. Because Ghandi was adept in Brahmanism, he was called Mahatma. _____

24. When she had a marrow bone, she made a rich soup it was delicious. _____

25. Architecture, in a general way, can be called frozen music. _____

36 DETECTING DISAGREEMENTS OF SUBJECT AND VERB

Section 13, *Essentials of English*

In some of the sentences below, the subjects and verbs agree; in others they do not. If the sentence is correct, write *C* in the space to the right. If the subject and verb do not agree, enclose the subject word in parentheses and write the correct verb form in the space to the right.

EXAMPLES:

Each of the incubators is kept at the same temperature.   C

The (schedule) of hours and assignments have been misplaced.   has

1. Neither of the jellies are clear. _____

2. Every candidate has been tested and several has already been appointed. _____

3. Some of the convicts has escaped. _____

4. A band of gypsies has been camping here. _____

5. Neither the omelet nor the cereal was edible. _____

6. Our greatest joy are our children. _____

7. None of the tubes have been tested. _____

8. Two-thirds of black college students is enrolled in predominantly white institutions. _____

9. Our greatest problem this year is the Japanese beetles. _____

10. A school of dolphins were sighted near the jetty. _____

11. Every policy and every contract have been carefully scrutinized. _____

12. In this poem the rhythm and the meter is awry. _____

13. The statistics have been compiled carefully.   _____

14. *Romeo and Juliet* is frequently performed.   _____

15. Neither of the wills have been properly drawn.   _____

16. Azalea is one of those plants that was once considered a botanical genus.   _____

17. In the lake there is two large islands.   _____

18. Twenty years are a harsh sentence for that crime.   _____

19. The barracks built as temporary structures in 1942 are still standing.   _____

20. Because of civil disturbances the legion were recalled to Rome.   _____

21. In this district our greatest problem are the undernourished and diseased
    children.   _____

22. In this period of repression, where is the men of principle?   _____

23. The major, as well as several non-commissioned officers, were charged with
    black market operations.   _____

24. Neither the washing machine nor the dryer is rated satisfactory.   _____

25. *The Birds* is the title of a play by Aristophanes.   _____

37 MAKING THE SUBJECT AND VERB AGREE

Section 13, *Essentials of English*

Each of the sentences below contains two forms of one verb. Find the subject of the verb and then choose the form of the verb which agrees with it. Write both the subject and the correct form of the verb in the spaces to the right. If the verb is governed by two or more subjects, write both of them in the appropriate space.

	Subject	Verb
EXAMPLES:		
Every article (has, have) been inspected.	article	has
The road and the driveway (need, needs) repair.	road and driveway	need

1. A selection of his short poems (has, have) been made for publication.

2. (Do, does) economics interest you?

3. Allison, Twist and Turner, Inc. (was, were) the successful bidder.

4. (Doesn't, don't) the vestrymen support the bishop?

5. He is one of the three youths who (was, were) chosen to accompany Admiral Byrd.

6. There (is, are) several reasons for blaming him.

7. Eight percent of the food (is, are) spoiled.

8. (Has, have) half of the foundation been dug?

9. The wages of sin (is, are) death.

10. (Has, have) the wages of office workers risen in this quarter?

11. (Is, are) international news adequately covered by our rural press?

12. (Was, were) the team arguing about who should be their captain?

13. Do you agree that the children (is, are) the hope of the world?

14. Her one pleasure (was, were) her beautiful dresses.

15. Her beautiful dresses (was, were) her one pleasure.

16. His tax refund, together with the little he manages to save, (covers, cover) the cost of his vacation.

17. Neither the president nor his advisors (has, have) acted wisely in this crisis.

18. Either the cloth or the dyes (is, are) defective.

19. Every tree and every shrub (has, have) been blighted.

20. A band of partisans (is, are) harassing our lines.

21. The miners of West Virginia and Pennsylvania (is, are) suffering from unemployment.

22. (Is, are) there many kinds of game in this area?

23. Some of the butter (is, are) rancid.

24. Most of the apples (is, are) wormy.

25. There (is, are) several strong reasons for discontinuing production.

38 MAKING THE SUBJECT AND VERB AGREE

Section 13, *Essentials of English*

Each of the sentences below contains two forms of one verb. Find the subject of the verb and then choose the form of the verb which **agrees** with it. Write both the subject and the correct form of the verb in the spaces to the right. If the verb is governed by two or more subjects, write all of them in the appropriate space.

EXAMPLES:

	Subject	Verb
Every article (has, have) been inspected.	article	has
The road and the driveway (needs, need) repair.	road and driveway	need

1. Twice a year the council (holds, hold) a public meeting.

2. There (has, have) been no objections to the proposed loan.

3. The President, guarded by secret service men, (takes, take) a brisk walk every morning.

4. To the economist statistics (is, are) an important subject.

5. To the economist a knowledge of statistics (is, are) important.

6. Each of the elementary schools (is, are) equipped with a gymnasium.

7. A package of food (is, are) sent each month.

8. One of our most popular designs (is, are) the snowflake.

9. Which of the two proposals (has, have) been accepted?

10. Here (lies, lie) the soldiers and sailors of the last war.

11. Most of the accounts (has, have) been audited. _____ _____

12. All of the trans-Atlantic planes (is, are) jets. _____ _____

13. The supervisor and several of the inspectors (has, have) been indicted for bribery. _____ _____

14. The supervisor, together with several inspectors, (has, have) been indicted for bribery. _____ _____

15. (Has, have) either Perkins and Company or Paul Fleischer Associates submitted a bid? _____ _____

16. A successful wife, mother, and career woman (is, are) what she wants to be. _____ _____

17. Exceptions (is, are) the test of the rule. _____ _____

18. The test of the rule (is, are) the exceptions. _____ _____

19. When (do, does) the bus leave for Albany? _____ _____

20. For adult males mumps (is, are) a serious disease. _____ _____

39 AGREEMENT OF PRONOUN AND ANTECEDENT

Section 14, *Essentials of English*

In each of the sentences below, two or more pronouns are placed in parentheses. Select the pronoun which agrees with the antecedent and write it in the space to the right.

EXAMPLE:

The visitor remained in (his, their) seat.   his

1. Will everyone please have (their, his or her) ticket ready?

2. The students are ready to settle (its, their) differences.

3. The police and the fire departments have abandoned (its, their) efforts to rescue the child from the mine.

4. Neither the child nor his parents have returned (his, their) books to the library.

5. The cat carried (his, her, its) kittens into the house.

6. The team won (its, their) greatest victory in 1956.

7. Has either Mary or Alice given (her, their) reasons for resigning from the club?

8. Neither the speakers nor the moderator did (his, their) best to explore the question.

9. Neither the moderator nor the speakers did (his, their) best to explore the question.

10. Some large animal has left (its, his) tracks in the mud behind the house.

11. The Board of Supervisors has consented to continue the hearing until every registered spokesman has the opportunity to voice (his, her, their, his or her) opinion.

12. Childhood is the time to have measles because (it, they) can be quite dangerous to an adult.

13. When anybody applies for a position, (he, he or she, they) must be sent to the personnel office.

14. It is impossible for a man to be cheated by anyone but (himself, themselves).

_____

15. Every sweet has its sour; every evil (its, their) good.

_____

16. The youth of the nation must receive (its, their) due.

_____

17. Ownership of property has (its, their) duties as well as rights.

_____

18. The masses of our countrymen are eager to clasp hands across the bloody chasm that has divided (it, them).

_____

19. Every man at last meets (his, their) Waterloo.

_____

20. A man is used as (he, they) uses others.

_____

21. All will be judged by (his, her, their) actions.

_____

22. Every man is like the company (he, they) is accustomed to keep.

_____

23. Consider the little mouse: how sagacious it is never to trust (his, its) life to one hole only.

_____

24. This and a great deal more like (it, them) I have had to put up with.

_____

25. No one knows what (he, he or she, they) can do until a time of trial.

_____

40 AGREEMENT OF PRONOUN AND ANTECEDENT

Section 14, *Essentials of English*

In each of the sentences below two or more pronouns are placed in parentheses. Select the pronoun which agrees with the antecedent and write it in the space to the right.

EXAMPLE:

The visitor remained in (his, their) seat.   his

1. The fire department and the underwriters have completed (its, their) investigation of the disaster.

2. The water and the smoke have done (its, their) damage.

3. The wealthy cannot buy (his, his or her, their) way to happiness.

4. Either Mr. Taub or Mr. Jamison may take (his, their) vacation in July.

5. Neither the landlord nor the tenants have filed (his, their) briefs.

6. Neither the guards nor the warden admits (his, their) responsibility for the disturbance.

7. All of the tenants have received (his or her, their) notice of eviction.

8. The committee will begin (its, their) investigation next week.

9. Every dog has (his, her, its) day.

10. The ocean liner sailed up the bay, every one of (its, her) pennants flying.

11. The native hunters tracked the animal to (its, his, her) lair.

12. Have all of you sent (his or her, their, your) contribution to the Community Fund?

13. The company was glad to hear that (its, their) captain would be court-martialed.

14. Neither of the boys has done (his, their) work properly.

15. Are all of the students ready for (his, their) tests?

16. Will either Mrs. Peabody or Mrs. Hamlin lend us (her, their) basket for the picnic?

17. When will the *Aspasia* sail on (his, her, its) maiden voyage?

18. Justice Alfred Dingle was the only one of the justices who expressed (his, their) disapproval of the procedure.

19. He is dabbling in politics to see if (they, it) appeals to him.

20. Neither of the brothers thought that (his, their) share of the estate was large enough.

21. Some alumna left (his, her, their) umbrella in the meeting room.

22. Dr. Margaret Crouse was one of the surgeons who donated (her, their) time to the clinic.

23. The Dulci Beauty Salon has added Miss Lenora to (its, their) staff.

24. Each of the men who worked on the project deserves to have (his, their) efforts commended.

25. Many a woman has sacrificed (her, their) husband for (her, their) children.

41 CORRECTING DISAGREEMENTS OF PRONOUN AND ANTECEDENT

Section 14, *Essentials of English*

Each of the following sentences contains a disagreement of pronoun and antecedent. Enclose the antecedent in parentheses and write the correct pronoun in the space to the right.

EXAMPLE:

I believe that every (man) has a right to their opinion.   his

1. Both of these poets have written sonnets about his courtship.

2. Each of the girls is required to make their own dress.

3. Neither the coach nor the trainer has submitted their resignation.

4. Anyone who called this play morbid and perverse must be out of their mind.

5. Neither the speakers nor the moderator can be praised for their contribution to the discussion.

6. Both Mr. Carstairs and Mr. Wilkins have offered his assistance.

7. Neither Mrs. Carstairs nor Mrs. Wilkins has offered their assistance.

8. Time is a river of passing events, and strong is their current.

9. The happiness and unhappiness of a rational, social animal depends on their deeds.

10. Many a worthy man has survived their own reputation.

11. Man is likely to believe what is least understandable to them.

12. Neither wealth nor a good reputation has bound him with their tentacles.

13. The staff expressed their confidence in the medical director.

14. The staff settled down at its desks.

15. Unanimously the faculty expressed their disapproval of the proposed changes in the curriculum. _____

16. Alice and Mary may leave her children with us. _____

17. When major international problems arise, we hope the United Nations will be able to solve it. _____

18. So closely related are the sublime and the ridiculous that it is often difficult to class it separately. _____

19. He said that these men, like Washington, are first in war, first in peace, and first in the hearts of his countrymen. _____

20. My little girl read *The Bobbsey Twins*, but she didn't like them. _____

21. Let every man be fully persuaded in their own mind. _____

22. Every unhappy family is unhappy in their own way. _____

23. Locked doors, guards, and all the trapping of hopeless confinement have been abolished because it deprived the patient of a sense of dignity. _____

24. In addition to his medical books, Keats kept a heavily marked copy of Shakespeare in his library, where they may be seen today. _____

25. Geoffrey Bates is among the employees who used up all his vacation time. _____

42 CORRECTING DISAGREEMENTS OF PRONOUN AND ANTECEDENT

Section 14, *Essentials of English*

Each of the following sentences contains a disagreement of pronoun and antecedent. Enclose the antecedent in parentheses and write the correct pronoun in the space to the right.

EXAMPLE:

No (woman) would take their troubles to him.   her

1. Many authors and thinkers have value even when wrong because it prompts us to think for ourselves.

2. Many a man is not a thinker because their memory is too good.

3. History repeats herself.

4. He watched the hen gather its chicks.

5. They call Fortune a woman because it is fickle.

6. Treat all your friends as if he or she might become your enemies.

7. If an actor is a hit in a particular role, directors are apt to typecast them.

8. As the Pied Piper marched through the streets, accompanied by a throng of children, the burghers watched them with alarm.

9. He is reading widely in aesthetics because he finds them interesting.

10. He dropped his course in economics because he found them too difficult.

11. In an emergency either Mrs. Cook or Mrs. Werbell will gladly volunteer their services.

12. Company B of the 116th Infantry is rightly proud of their citation for distinguished service.

13. Channel 13 is justifiably proud of their programming.

One way to avoid problems of gender is to recast sentences so that both the pronouns and their antecedents are in the plural. In the following sentences, enclose the pronouns and antecedents in parentheses, and write the plural forms in the spaces to the right.

EXAMPLE:

	Antecedent	Pronoun
Each police officer will report to his or her precinct immediately.	All police officers	their

14. Each student will bring his or her books to class.

15. A doctor specializing in research may find that he or she lacks a bedside manner.

16. The organization aided every Tuscarora Indian in his resistance to the state government.

17. Whoever is beautiful has the source of beauty within himself.

18. A lawyer must rely on the good faith of his clients.

19. A job applicant must provide a resume giving his or her qualifications.

20. A parent may not always know what is best for his or her children.

43 IDENTIFYING PRONOUNS AND ANTECEDENTS

Section 15, *Essentials of English*

In each of the following sentences you are to identify the pronoun, find its antecedent, and write both of them in the appropriate spaces to the right. If the pronoun refers to two or more antecedents, write them in the appropriate space. If the antecedent is not clear, write *vague* in the appropriate space.

EXAMPLES:

	Pronoun	Antecedent
I know the reason, but it escapes me now.	it	reason
Wood, whiskey, and cheese improve when they are properly aged.	they	wood, whiskey cheese
The captain told the lieutenant that he had made a miscalculation.	he	vague

1. The coach reminded the quarterback that he was responsible for the team. _____ _____

2. Let the man who is without fault cast the first stone. _____ _____

3. They followed the trail which the scouts had blazed through the forest. _____ _____

4. Quarles was the agent who represented the Indians. _____ _____

5. The craftsman labors for his living. _____ _____

6. If a man buys a thing to sell whole and unchanged, he is a merchant. _____ _____

7. Medicine affords the opportunity to serve and to earn, which is why John wants to be a doctor. _____ _____

8. The hailstones pelted the top of the automobile; they were as big as mothballs. _____ _____

9. Mary would make a good nurse, but that is an arduous profession. _____ _____

10. Every dog has its day. _____ _____

11. Lewis Carroll, who wrote *Alice in Wonderland,* was a mathematician.

12. The boys and girls may invite their parents to visit the science fair.

    _____   _____

13. Throughout the country many old people live with children or relatives who are indigent.

    _____   _____

14. Father assembled the storage chest with ease, which surprised him greatly.

    _____   _____

15. In the stacks were hundreds of books with leather bindings that were damp and torn.

    _____   _____

16. The oppressions of the tyrannous landlord who used economic power to drive a hard bargain were the subject of continual denunciation.

    _____   _____

17. The Bible, the Schoolmen, the Fathers, the church councils—all these were quoted as decisive on economic questions involving ethics.

    _____   _____

18. Sermons and pamphlets do not deal with sins that no one commits.

    _____   _____

19. The most striking quality of this teaching is its conservatism.

    _____   _____

20. During the debate, both candidates were trying to avoid the issue, and this clearly irritated the moderator.

    _____   _____

21. Ravel's *Bolero* became so popular that he was surprised.

    _____   _____

22. These retarded children show marked improvement when they are properly nurtured and provided with opportunities to see and do and learn.

    _____   _____

23. Hyperbole is a figure of speech that makes a gross exaggeration, but without any intent to deceive.

    _____   _____

24. *Buddenbrooks* is the novel that made Thomas Mann famous at the age of twenty-five.

    _____   _____

25. He wanted me to co-sign a note for him, which I did.

    _____   _____

44 IDENTIFYING PRONOUNS AND ANTECEDENTS

Section 15, *Essentials of English*

In each of the following sentences you are to identify the pronoun, find its antecedent, and write both of them in the appropriate spaces to the right. If the pronoun refers to two or more antecedents, write them in the appropriate space. If the antecedent is not clear, write *vague* in the appropriate space.

EXAMPLES:

	Pronoun	Antecedent
I know the reason, but it escapes me now.	it	reason
Wood, whiskey, and cheese improve when they are properly aged.	they	wood whiskey cheese
The captain told the lieutenant that he had made a miscalculation.	he	vague

1. The telephone company promised that it would restore service at once.

2. The picnickers lost their way in the state forest.

3. She can sing G above high C, which is phenomenal.

4. Mr. Sweet's travelogue is so interesting and informative that he has won an award.

5. Most of the people who live in Coatsville are immigrants.

6. Marsland Sparrow is the attorney whom the accused has engaged.

7. On the day after Labor Day the beach was closed, which was a surprise to the summer renters.

8. Bob told Tom that Smith had stolen his catcher's mitt.

9. Mrs. Maloney is one of the commuters who get on the train at Syosset.

10. Since Merino's bid was the lowest, he was engaged. _____ _____

11. Since Merino made the lowest bid, he was engaged. _____ _____

12. Consider the lilies of the field, how they grow. _____ _____

13. Give a man a horse he can ride. _____ _____

14. The people upstairs bring friends in and dance, and this goes on every night. _____ _____

15. The shop steward reminded the foreman that he was once an unskilled worker. _____ _____

16. The singing commercial was so clever and catchy that it became a popular song. _____ _____

17. Charles Lamb feared that he might become mad. _____ _____

18. McKenzie is the leader whom the rank-and-file members trust. _____ _____

19. Mrs. Maloney is the only one of the commuters who gets on the train at Syosset. _____ _____

20. In today's paper it describes the havoc wrought by the earthquake in Italy. _____ _____

45 CASE OF NOUNS AND PRONOUNS

Section 16, *Essentials of English*

Each of the following sentences contains two cases of the same pronoun or two different ways of indicating case. Choose the correct form and write it in the space to the right.

EXAMPLES:

They thought that the winner was (I, me). _____ I

1. It was (they, them) who donated the draperies.

   _____

2. He believed that the culprit was (I, me).

   _____

3. All of the interested people, (we, us) residents of Hedgerow Lane, must protest the regulation.

   _____

4. Our Japanese gardener taught (her, she) all that she knows about the art of folding paper.

   _____

5. That is for (we, us), the citizens of the town, to decide.

   _____

6. Just between you and (I, me), I think the design for the new town hall is much too elaborate.

   _____

7. The girls next door were so pretty that we wanted to be like (they, them).

   _____

8. The children are naughty, but scolding (they, them) does no good.

   _____

9. The James boys are so big and strong that we want (they, them) to be color guards.

   _____

10. Mrs. Winfield Terwilliger and (her, she) were named the best dressed women of the year.

    _____

11. The Judge excused Laughlin from jury duty as well as (I, me).

    _____

12. Let him orchestrate the melody because he knows more about theory than (I, me).

    _____

13. Since you have more confidence in Jones than (I, me), let's transfer him from my department to yours.

14. Mr. Anderson did not recommend him as highly as he did (I, me).

15. Place the stake midway between him and (I, me).

16. Let us divide the canvassing between (us, we) selectmen.

17. (Who, Whom) was that satirical column about?

18. (Who, Whom) wrote that satirical column?

19. (Who, Whom) does he think denounced him to the investigating committee?

20. (Who, Whom) did the editor ask the special feature writer to interview for our next issue?

21. A box at the opera is much too expensive for someone like (I, me).

22. I will not take the blame for (somebody, somebody's) pilfering.

23. I will not take the blame for (somebody, somebody's) in the office pilfering from the petty cash box.

24. (Who, Whom) do you think you are?

25. The people (who, whom) I see at the airport are always in a hurry.

46 CASE OF NOUNS AND PRONOUNS

Section 16, *Essentials of English*

Each of the following sentences contains two cases of the same pronoun or two different ways of indicating case. Choose the correct form and write it in the space to the right.

EXAMPLES:

They thought that the winner was (I, me).   I

1. The (girl, girl's) chewing gum is the new secretary.

2. It was (they, them) who were loitering in front of the liquor store.

3. In the line-up she identified (he, him) as her assailant.

4. For (pity, pity's) sake help me shovel this walk.

5. When she heard about (John, John's) winning first prize in the contest, she was astounded.

6. When she heard about (John, John's), her son-in-law, winning first prize, she was astounded.

7. It was (I, me) who opened the store this morning.

8. They thought it was (I, me) in the news photograph.

9. The rescue crew arrived to find (him, his) holding on to the branch of a tree on the edge of the cliff.

10. The victims of the swindle, (us, we) stockholders, must engage an attorney to represent us.

11. (Him, his) grabbing hold of a branch of the tree at the edge of a cliff was the only thing that saved him.

12. We even tried praising (he, him), but praise did no good.

_____

13. Mr. Sampson and (I, me) volunteered to write the petition.

_____

14. Mr. Sampson wrote the petition because he has a better command of the language than (I, me).

_____

15. (Who, Whom) is the board considering for the presidency of the Newton Home for the Aged?

_____

16. (Who, Whom) do you think she will name as corespondent?

_____

17. (Who, Whom) do you consider to be the better composer, Schubert or Schumann?

_____

18. (Who, Whom) is the better composer, Schubert or Schumann?

_____

19. Blame (whoever, whomever) took the message without asking for the caller's name.

_____

20. She is her (husbands, husband's) drinking companion.

_____

21. The (bird, bird's) singing in the apple tree is an oriole.

_____

22. We were kept awake all night by the (dog, dog's) barking.

_____

23. We were kept awake all night by the (dog, dog's) in the garage next door barking.

_____

24. Do Karen, Michelle, and (I, me) have to stay?

_____

25. I received the appointment because on the test I scored higher than (they, them).

_____

47 CORRECTING ERRORS IN CASE

Section 16, *Essentials of English*

Many of the following sentences contain a noun or pronoun in the wrong case. Enclose each faulty noun or pronoun in parentheses and write the correct form in the space to the right. If the sentence is correct, write *C* in the space to the right.

EXAMPLES:

(Whom) do you believe will win the election?   who
_____

You are no taller than she.   C
_____

1. While I was speaking to you, whom do you think might have over-heard our conversation?
_____

2. Mother is opposed to Henry wrestling on the high school team.
_____

3. They disapproved of us calling the police to complain about the disturbance.
_____

4. It was we who were most disturbed.
_____

5. I am a faster stenographer than she, but she is more accurate than I.
_____

6. The agreement must be kept a secret between you and I.
_____

7. Awards were presented to three boys in our school, Gregory Thiele, Joe Mersey, and I.
_____

8. Everybody in this town is mad, excluding you and I of course.
_____

9. They asked us girls to act as ushers.
_____

10. Joan and Mary were suspected of stealing the money, but not her.
_____

11. Mrs. Shaw called to ask me who I would recommend as soprano soloist in the church choir.
_____

12. Whom do you think they are talking about, you or me?
_____

13. I am not as scornful of jazz as them. _____

14. In fact, I appreciate jazz far more than them. _____

15. They do not like us as much as we like them. _____

16. We think them to be the boys who are stealing our apples. _____

17. Father established trust funds for us children, Fred, Louise, and I. _____

18. Father established trust funds for we children, Fred, Louise, and me. _____

19. Among the three of us boys, Milton, Pancho, and me, we had less than two dollars. _____

20. The chairman objected to Mary, who sat in the first row, knitting throughout the entire discussion. _____

21. The chairman objected to Mary knitting, no matter where she sat. _____

22. I want to thank you for the lovely basket of fruit from Florida that you sent to Mr. Green and I. _____

23. I will give the dress to she who looks most attractive in it. _____

24. It was he, not me, who won the raffle. _____

25. It was him, not I, who won the raffle. _____

48 CORRECTING ERRORS IN CASE

Section 16, *Essentials of English*

Many of the following sentences contain a noun or pronoun in the wrong case. Enclose the faulty noun or pronoun in parentheses and write the correct form in the space to the right. If the sentence is correct, write *C* in the space to the right.

EXAMPLES:

(Whom) do you believe will win the election?   who

You are no taller than she.   C

1. May us boys swim in the pool?   _____

2. Will Mr. Barnes let us boys swim in the pool?   _____

3. Did Mr. Barnes say that us boys may swim in the pool?   _____

4. We do not have a hundred dollars between us and bankruptcy.   _____

5. He wants to swim as well as Jim—the county champion—and me.   _____

6. No matter what anyone thinks, we know that it is them who are at fault.   _____

7. He is convinced that it was they, the Martins, who borrowed the book.   _____

8. Everyone expected they to be the winners of the bridge tournament.   _____

9. He requested they to be the godparents of his first child.   _____

10. May us girls, as well as the boys, swim in Mr. Barnes' pool?   _____

11. Mr. Barnes said that us girls may swim in his pool.   _____

12. We girls, Sue, Molly, and I, want to do something to express our appreciation to Mr. Barnes.   _____

13. Who invented the typewriter?

_____

14. By whom was the typewriter invented?

_____

15. Whom do you think invented the typewriter?

_____

16. Please use this money for the child whom you think most needs a vacation.

_____

17. Who shall I say telephoned?

_____

18. It was she who made the motion to adjourn.

_____

19. They are richer than us.

20. John is more talented than he, and he is more ambitious and industrious than I.

_____

21. I would like to be him.

_____

22. I want to be like him.

_____

23. Did you take him to be I ?

_____

24. Sympathy should be expressed for we parents who make the sacrifices.

_____

25. Who will bring the cold cuts, you or me ?

_____

49 DETECTING DANGLING MODIFIERS

Section 17, *Essentials of English*

Some of the following sentences are correct; others contain a dangling modifier. Write *C* in the space to the right of each correct sentence. Opposite each sentence containing a dangling modifier write *D* and enclose the dangling modifier in parentheses.

EXAMPLES:

(While rowing in shallow water),the boat struck a flat rock.   D

On examining his account, he discovered the discrepancy.   C

1. To be tender and digestible you must boil an egg for twenty minutes.   _____

2. To become a law the president must sign a bill.   _____

3. After passing both houses of congress, a bill must be signed by the president in order to become a law.   _____

4. By signing a bill, the president makes it a law.   _____

5. After serving in the Senate for sixteen years, the chairmanship was his.   _____

6. Our millionaires did not become rich by saving their money.   _____

7. By scrimping and saving for five years, the trip abroad was a possibility at last.   _____

8. The journey was too arduous to undertake.   _____

9. To hook a rug, patience is required.   _____

10. While representing the Apex Corporation in Rome, the Pope granted him an audience.   _____

11. After allowing the canoe to dry thoroughly, you must scrape and paint it.   _____

12. After failing for years, success was finally his.   _____

13. Lowering the shades, the room was plunged into darkness.

14. Having been convicted of drunken driving, the Bureau of Motor Vehicles revoked his license. _____

15. By providing his own power line, the landlord permitted him to operate an air conditioner. _____

16. As the greatest golfer of all, I have chosen Bobby Jones. _____

17. By using animated cartoons and other visual aids, the principle of atomic energy was made clear. _____

18. Upon learning that I was ill in the hospital, I received many visits from my lodge brothers. _____

19. Square dancing has become popular in the last few years. _____

20. In diagnosing certain illnesses, the patient's medical history must be considered. _____

21. Being an alien, the position was not given to him. _____

22. While driving through the Southwest, the aridity and desolation are oppressive. _____

23. In order to achieve a goal, one must be prepared to work and sacrifice. _____

24. In order to teach a person, he must be willing to learn. _____

25. At last, after working for days, the lawn was free of crab grass. _____

50 CORRECTING DANGLING MODIFIERS

Section 17, *Essentials of English*

Each of the following sentences contains a dangling modifier. Enclose the dangling modifier in parentheses and rewrite the sentence to make it clear.

EXAMPLE:

(While tying my shoe), the lace broke.

While I was tying my shoe, the lace broke.

1. To be mellow and subtle in taste, you must process a wine with care.

   _____

2. To be sweet and mild, you must clean a pipe regularly.

   _____

3. While searching through bundles of unclassified periodicals in the Library of Congress, a new photograph of Lincoln was discovered.

   _____

4. For a moment, while looking at me sorrowfully, there was a resemblance to my father.

   _____

5. In order to sell a man insurance, he must be reminded of his responsibilities to his family.

   _____

6. In comparing these two hearing aids, they seem to be equally sensitive.

   _____

7. Though musical and facile at the piano, the judges thought that the child was emotionally immature.

   _____

8. While painting *Guernica,* I believe that Picasso was not in control of his emotions.

   _____

9. To receive a reply to your inquiry, a self-addressed envelope must be enclosed.

   _____

10. By comparing these two specimens under the microscope, their similarities are readily apparent.

_____

11. Born and raised in Ireland, his brogue never left him.

_____

12. His teeth were stained with nicotine from smoking too many cigarettes.

_____

13. Played with exquisite musicianship, Mr. Bohun was pleased with Tchaikowsky's piano concerto for the first time.

_____

14. To get a passport, a non-communist oath is no longer necessary.

_____

15. Holding two full-time jobs, there was no time for leisure and recreation.

_____

16. Reading the poetry of Dylan Thomas, the music of the language intoxicated him.

_____

17. His business was jeopardized by granting credit too readily.

_____

18. Though replete with beautiful passages and well-conceived characters, the editor rejected the novel.

_____

19. While learning to play tennis as a boy, my father practiced with me.

_____

20. In order to be an entertainer, projection is required.

_____

51 MISPLACED MODIFIERS

Section 18, *Essentials of English*

In each of the following sentences identify the misplaced modifier by enclosing it in parentheses. In the appropriate space write the word which the modifier should immediately precede. If the modifier should be placed at the end of the sentence, write *E* in the appropriate space.

EXAMPLE:

He offered to paint the fence (last night), and I hope he will do it.

He _____

1. Kevin O'Dempsey wanted to be a priest when he was a boy.

_____

2. The plague almost killed a fifth of the population.

_____

3. He demanded retribution in a shrill voice.

_____

4. While working for a chartered accountant on the advice of his doctor he decided to study medicine.

_____

5. Father only rooted up the poison ivy.

_____

6. Disraeli charmed the Queen with a solicitous and courtly air.

_____

7. The telethon almost raised a hundred thousand dollars for multiple sclerosis.

_____

8. His writing is pallid because it only depicts virtue, bravery, and beauty.

_____

9. Bacon's campaign against excessive rationalism raised him above those who merely pleaded for science or freedom of thought.

_____

10. At first the Copernican theory was unacceptable because it obliterated chiefly the distinction between corruptible and incorruptible.

_____

11. The pediatrician and the accountant began to realize that they could always stay sober that evening and be helped by helping others to stay sober.

_____

12. His formulas are easier to understand no doubt than any of the others.

_____

13. In some cases where the Supreme Court has upheld claims of civil liberties, though divided, the decisions have been within the area of legitimate difference of opinion.

14. He realized that experimentation did not appeal to him after attending the institute for a semester.

<u>   </u>

15. The heretic was told that if he did not instantly recant within a week he would be excommunicated.

<u>   </u>

16. Keats realized before his pen had gleaned his teeming brain that he might die.

<u>   </u>

17. In his retirement Judge Flacks wrote an exposé of Boss Tweed and Tammany Hall based on his personal experience.

<u>   </u>

18. The management consultant declared that if the business were not quickly reorganized within two years it would be bankrupt.

<u>   </u>

19. One teacher only seems to have influenced him.

<u>   </u>

20. There only remained one source from which the Protestant poet could draw images and fables that were poetic and true: the Bible.

<u>   </u>

52 DETECTING MIXED AND SPLIT CONSTRUCTIONS

Section 19, *Essentials of English*

In the space to the right of each of the following sentences write *M* if the sentence contains a mixed construction, *S* if it contains a split construction, and *C* if it is correct.

EXAMPLES:

There is no one to whom he can apply to for help.	M
He wanted to swiftly sink through the floor.	S
Our teacher used to say that there is no royal road to geometry.	C

1. An applicant for a job must consider how can he best state his qualifications.

2. What the dentist could not guarantee was how long would the teeth support the crowns.

3. His parents ordered him to stay out of deep water until he can swim better.

4. The problem to be solved was how could the fragile glass be packed for shipping?

5. The Haymarket riot in Chicago was the result of a mass protest against the killing of strikers by the police.

6. The Huntington Library and Art Gallery is situated in San Marino, California.

7. The Hessians were mercenary soldiers who were hired by Great Britain during the Revolutionary War.

8. Hiawatha, a Mohawk, was one of the medicine men responsible for, in time of common danger, the organization of the Iroquois Confederacy.

9. The Hopi Indians inhabit six pueblos living in northeastern Arizona.

10. The Massachusetts Bay Colony was organized for, as a counterpart to Virginia, trading and settlement.

11. As students the Wesleys wanted to without reservations accept the teachings of the Church of England.

12. The minstrel show was a type of variety entertainment presenting white men in black face which, although originating in the United States, it became popular in Europe.

13. Early motion pictures were exhibited as curiosities in vaudeville houses or at make-shift theatres called nickelodeons.

        _____

14. He was pleased to remember who were the leading members of the "Brain Trust."

        _____

15. To quiet industrial unrest in the East was why the Homestead Act was adopted.

        _____

16. Pinkerton prevented, in 1861, an attempted assassination of Lincoln.

17. Franklin Delano Roosevelt, the thirty-second president of the United States, was elected to four terms of office.

        _____

18. Prohibition, the legal prevention of the manufacture and sale of alcoholic beverages, was a result of the temperance movement.

        _____

19. The reason he came to see us so often was because he enjoyed talking to my father about politics.

        _____

20. The newspaper correspondent asked the candidate would he repudiate his radical supporters.

        _____

21. Paul Revere's own account of his celebrated ride is contained in, as few people know, a letter to Jeremy Belknap.

        _____

22. The United States is awarded two Rhodes Scholarships for each state and territory.

        _____

23. The Brooklyn Bridge was planned by John Roebling, a pioneer in the construction of suspension bridges.

        _____

24. Roebling's death as the result of an accident was why he did not complete the Brooklyn Bridge.

        _____

25. In the museum he was most impressed by, among the abstract paintings, the work of Jackson Pollock.

        _____

53 DETECTING SPLIT CONSTRUCTIONS

Section 19, *Essentials of English*

Some of the following sentences are correct and some contain a split construction. If the sentence is correct, write C in the space to the right. If the sentence contains a split construction, enclose the misplaced element in parentheses and write *split* in the space to the right.

EXAMPLES:

I am unable to (honestly) say that I like a sheath dress.   split

If you have the time, you must begin to read more widely.   C

1. Our representative must be able to fluently speak Spanish. _____

2. Dreaming that the spirit of Schubert had brought him a theme, Schumann rushed out of bed to quickly write it down. _____

3. The drama of alcoholism is less exciting than the attempts to deeply plumb its sources. _____

4. History and headlines have conditioned us to think of our differences with the U.S.S.R. in terms of power balances and prolonged conflicts. _____

5. Our foreign policy and our defense policy will be no doubt issues in the next presidential election. _____

6. We sometimes perceive, in our childhood, hidden influences that have affected the course of our lives. _____

7. Examining the X-ray, the internist saw in the duodenal region a cloudy mass. _____

8. He drew attention, with a discreet cough, to his presence. _____

9. The shipment of buckles would arrive by, your salesman promised, the first of the month. _____

10. Every society needs leaders to help solve its problems and to clarify its better impulses. _____

11. Many people believe that it is not for a judge, but for legislators to enact into law the public's conscience. _____

12. For the exhibition the judges selected only those pictures, as I knew they would, which were representational. _____

13. A great deal of information on defense matters is, as our enemies know, made available in congressional hearings.

14. Thousands of men lost their fortunes when the stock market crashed and millions lost their jobs.

15. There is scarcely a general in the Pentagon who would recommend our present course of defense or an expert in the scientific aspects of defense.

16. The witness identified, to everybody's surprise, the defense attorney as the man she had seen driving away from the scene of the crime.

17. They drove for miles and miles, looking for, in that remote section of Utah, a motel where they could spend the night.

18. Although Job was sorely tempted to, by his afflictions and his comforters, curse God, he resisted the temptation.

19. The serpent tempted Eve to eat of the tree of knowledge.

20. When they heard the voice of the Lord, Adam and Eve were, in their nakedness, ashamed to appear before Him.

21. Hudson sailed up the river, thinking that he had, in this unexplored wilderness, found the northwest passage at last.

22. The Board of Directors threatened to at once discharge anyone who invoked the Fifth Amendment.

23. The Pilgrims landed on, as every schoolboy knows, Plymouth Rock in Massachusetts.

24. Paul Revere rode through the night to spread the alarm that the British were coming.

25. The East defeated with a burst of scoring in the final minutes the West in the NBA All-Star Game in 1980.

54 DETECTING INCOMPLETE AND ILLOGICAL COMPARISONS

Section 20, *Essentials of English*

Many of the following sentences contain incomplete or illogical comparisons. In the space to the right of each sentence write *C* if the sentence is correct and *W* if the sentence is wrong.

EXAMPLES:

I am stronger than he.   C

He is the smartest of any boy in his class.   W

1. Of the two, Betty is tallest.   _____

2. John is the tallest of the twins.   _____

3. In the quartet his voice is the best.   _____

4. Our team is as strong as theirs, if not stronger.   _____

5. Of all the states in the Union, Alaska and Hawaii are the newer. _____

6. He picked as many, if not more apples, than his father.   _____

7. She is older than any other mother on the block.   _____

8. He likes Helen better than Ruth.   _____

9. The population of London is larger than New York.   _____

10. He is the most successful merchant in town.   _____

11. That is the most disgusting advertisement on television.   _____

12. He is the most notorious of any gangster alive today.   _____

13. I like swimming in the ocean better than lakes.   _____

14. Mark is the middle child, and Jimmy is the older. _____

15. I like ice cream better than sherbet. _____

16. This machine is the most efficient typewriter on the market. _____

17. He is the most talented of any director in the theatre today. _____

18. John Dillinger was the most talented of any bank robber. _____

19. The pitcher likes the coach better than the athletic director. _____

20. I am as big, if not bigger than, my father. _____

21. Corn is better in August than September. _____

22. Asparagus is more delicious than any vegetable. _____

23. This pear is as sweet as sugar. _____

24. He is the best of any ballplayer playing today. _____

25. This melon is as green as grass. _____

55 INCOMPLETE AND ILLOGICAL COMPARISONS

Section 20, *Essentials of English*

Many of the following sentences contain incomplete or illogical comparisons. If the sentence is correct, write *C* in the space to the right. If the comparison is incomplete, write the word or words that should be added in the space to the right. If the comparison is illogical, enclose the word or words that should be omitted in parentheses and write them in the space to the right.

EXAMPLES:

He is as brown as a berry.	C
He is as wealthy, if not wealthier than, his uncle.	as
Tweed was the most corrupt (of any) politician of his day.	of any

1. Our jets are as fast, if not faster than, any Soviet planes.

2. Banlon keeps its shape better than any synthetic fabric.

3. Until recently Texas was bigger than any state in the Union.

4. Caruso was the most celebrated opera singer of modern times.

5. Antarctica has the coldest of any climate in the world.

6. James Joyce liked Yeats better than Synge.

7. For every kind of motoring these brakes are more reliable than any other automobile.

8. The Mississippi is larger than any other river in the United States.

9. I think that the Volkswagen is better than any American car.

10. In fact, I think that the Volkswagen is the best foreign car.

11. The giant redwoods are the tallest of any trees in North America.

12. Which is the largest of the Great Lakes?

13. Judging by its name, I would say that Lake Superior is the larger of the Great Lakes.

_____

14. Which mountains are tallest, the Alps or the Himalayas?

_____

15. In our basketball team the center is the better scorer.

_____

16. June is one of the loveliest months of the year.

17. He believes that the law is the most crowded of any profession in the United States.

_____

18. Medicine is no longer the most remunerative of all the other professions.

_____

19. Lincoln is more beloved than any American statesman or president.

_____

20. The system of roads in New Jersey is as good as any other state in the East.

_____

21. He thought much more highly of Theodore Roosevelt than Franklin Roosevelt.

_____

22. Queen Victoria trusted Disraeli more than Gladstone.

_____

23. The Rolls Royce was the most expensive automobile manufactured in the twentieth century.

_____

24. Social workers and teachers are unanimous in the belief that young people are more socially conscious than yesterday.

_____

25. I made two attempts, and the first was the best.

_____

56 SUPPLYING NECESSARY WORDS

Section 21, *Essentials of English*

From some of the following sentences one or more necessary words have been omitted. If necessary words have been omitted, write the omitted words in the space to the right. If the sentence is ambiguous, write *A* in the appropriate space. If the sentence is correct, write *C*.

EXAMPLES:

Reported late to work this morning because of accident.	I, an
He hired a nurse and housekeeper.	A
She is charming and is loved by everybody.	C

1. Brackets and screws have been omitted from the carton.

2. Was surprised by appearance of pigeon on sidewalk this morning.

3. The first stage show I ever saw was *Oklahoma!*

4. The music for *Oklahoma!* was written by Richard Rodgers, the libretto by Oscar Hammerstein.

5. For years she has been attended by a nurse and companion.

6. Was the success of his first novel due to his friend and editor?

7. Thomas Wolfe owed part of his success to his friend and editor, Max Perkins.

8. Despite his failure, we all have hope and faith in Arnold.

9. The kite flew high above the roofs of the houses and over the telegraph poles.

10. This tincture should be rubbed thoroughly into the hair and the scalp.

11. The United States always has and always will be a peace-loving nation.

12. He believes that we cannot rely on the United Nations or even NATO.

13. Before he was thirty, he controlled a bank and trust company.

_____

14. She is a talented actress and sought by many producers.

_____

15. Their home was designed by Theodore Brixon, of Brixon and Tuck, and their rooms furnished by Belle Pomerantz.

_____

16. In this hotel the rooms are luxurious and the cuisine delicious.

_____

17. They were defeated because their fortifications were weak and their strategy stupid.

_____

18. He decided to use the front room on the second floor as a bedroom and study.

_____

19. We children were never allowed to enter grandfather's bedroom and study.

_____

20. The union feared the company would close its factory and move to the South.

_____

21. Situations like these always have and probably always will be difficult to resolve.

_____

22. If they questioned me, I was instructed to answer their complaint had never been received.

_____

23. The teacher was conscientious and the students diligent.

_____

24. Changing economic conditions can lead to a decrease or increase in your profit margin.

_____

25. When he died, his business was liquidated by his son and heir.

_____

57 NECESSARY WORDS AND INCOMPLETE CONSTRUCTIONS

Section 21, *Essentials of English*

The following sentences are logically incomplete. Complete each sentence and write the revised sentence in the space below.

EXAMPLE:

Her new coat is too beautiful!

Her new coat is beautiful. *or* Her new coat is too beautiful for daily wear.

1. Life is too dreary!

   _____

2. I had such a difficult day!

   _____

3. These flowers are so beautiful!

   _____

4. He is just too honest!

   _____

5. Children are such ingrates!

   _____

6. The social director is so amusing!

   _____

7. He dances so gracefully!

   _____

8. The evening has been so delightful!

   _____

9. He is such a droll comedian!

_____

10. The day is so hot!

_____

A necessary word has been omitted from each of the following sentences. Write the omitted word in the space to the right.

EXAMPLE:

She has had brief roles in *Stolen Kisses* and *Skip to My Lou.*　　　　in

_____

11. He has gone abroad for the summer with his wife and mother.

_____

12. The builder has completed most of the houses and will the others by the end of August.

_____

13. The mice are kept in the laboratory on the roof and the sub-basement.

_____

14. The public seems to place little confidence or reliance on either of the leading candidates for mayor.

_____

15. Do you fear automation will produce mass unemployment?

_____

16. The notes are prolix and the index incomplete.

_____

17. We believe our new senator will work to improve the local economy.

_____

18. Do you notice how piles are refracted in the water?

_____

19. Son of a coal miner, D. H. Lawrence was proud of aristocratic wife, Frieda.

_____

20. With this new chemical we hope to kill all poison ivy around the camp.

_____

21. They left a generous tip for the waiter and bus boy.

_____

22. His chauffeur and gardener inherited his entire estate.

_____

23. The pitcher refuses to accept the contract, saying that he has and still can earn his living as a barber.

_____

24. This history underestimates the importance of the encounter of the *Monitor* and *Merrimac.*

_____

25. Captain Boycott, Irish land agent, has given us the term *boycott.*

_____

58 PARALLELISM

Section 22F, *Essentials of English*

Some of the following sentences present parallel ideas in parallel form; others do not. Mark C (correct) those sentences which use parallelism effectively. Mark X (wrong) those which do not.

EXAMPLES:

He liked hunting and to fish.   X

He liked hunting and fishing.   C

1. The article was short, informative, and reading it was easy. _____

2. The article was short, informative, and easy to read. _____

3. The order of business will be as follows:
   a. Calling the meeting to order
   b. Taking attendance
   c. Hearing reports from the standing committees
   d. Attending to new business
   e. Setting a date for the next meeting _____

4. The order of business will be as follows:
   a. Calling the meeting to order
   b. Rollcall
   c. The committees will report.
   d. New business
   e. A date should be set for the next meeting. _____

5. You don't have to be raised on a farm to be able to tell the difference between a young rooster and a female chicken that has reached old age. _____

6. You don't have to be raised on a farm to be able to tell the difference between a young rooster and an old hen. _____

7. He took the job because he needed money and because he wanted experience. _____

8. He took the job because he needed to earn some money and experience would be useful to him. _____

9. John worked on the farm in summer, and in the winter almost any job that came along seemed good enough for him. _____

10. John worked on the farm in summer and took anything he could get in winter. _____

115

11. The report should be in writing, not delivered orally. _____

12. He was fired because he was not interested in the job, the boss didn't like him, and laziness. _____

13. Many people prefer an honest idiot to a dishonest genius. _____

14. When you have swept the floor and the furniture is dusted, let me know. _____

15. He took his bicycle to the repair shop to get the brake adjusted, and the headlight didn't work very well. _____

16. When he was praised, he beamed; when he was scolded, he sulked. _____

17. It was a miserable climate: when the skies were clear, it was too hot for comfort; when it wasn't hot, it seemed as if it rained or there was fog all the time. _____

18. He picked up a book, turned on the light, and sat down to read. _____

19. Reading letters is a pleasure, but to write them is something few people enjoy doing. _____

20. He was not only anxious to make a good first impression, but he also hoped that people would keep right on liking him. _____

59 CONSISTENCY

Section 23, *Essentials of English*

One word or a group of connected words in each of the following exercises is inconsistent in number, person, or tense. Identify the inconsistent word or word-group by enclosing it in **parentheses**. Make the necessary correction in the space provided at the right.

EXAMPLE:

A person doesn't really know when he is well off until **(they have)** endured hardship.

he has

1. The horned toad is a short-legged, short-tailed lizard with spines along its back. Their body is wide and flat.

2. To replace a bicycle tire, you must first remove the wheel from the frame. Otherwise, you will not be able to get the old tire off or the new tire on. This seems like a very obvious procedure, but you would be surprised to know how many people pull off the tire without removing the wheel and then discovered that the tire is trapped by the axle.

3. The Hippocratic Oath is a pledge that was taken in classical times by young men who were studying medicine. The oath is still administered to graduates of medical schools before they receive their medical degrees. It was formerly believed that the oath was composed by Hippocrates, but recent research indicates that it was written at a later period. Among other things, the oath pledges the doctor to secrecy concerning the private affairs of his patients. It is therefore unethical for a doctor to discuss the personal affairs of his clients with anybody else, regardless of whether they are relatives or close personal friends.

4. If students wish to master an assignment, they should first read it through rapidly to get a general idea of the whole topic. Then they should go back and underline all the important points. Finally, they should make an outline of the topics, arranging them in logical order. You should follow this plan to achieve academic success.

5. Wild boars were first domesticated by the Chinese as early as 2900 B.C. In Europe they were domesticated at a considerably later date. The value of hogs was soon apparent. They not only provided excellent food, but they were easy to feed, and they also acted as wonderful disposers of garbage. Another reason for the popularity of hogs is that it reproduces more rapidly than most other edible animals.

   _____

6. You can do it easily if one is skillful.

   _____

7. Many a man in debt applies to a loan company with the odd idea that borrowing money from one agency to pay another is a solution to their money problems.

   _____

8. He ran to the edge of the lake, pulled off his clothes and jumps in with a tremendous splash.

   _____

9. Astrologers cast horoscopes to predict the future. If people want answers about particular problems, you can also ask specific questions. Both predictions and answers to specific questions are equally reliable.

   _____

10. The students were discussing a particularly difficult problem in mathematics when they heard a tremendous crash. The teacher sprang from her desk and ran to the window to look out. When she saw that it was only a pile of snow that had slipped off the roof, she turned to the class and explains what happened.

    _____

60 TERMINAL PUNCTUATION

Section 25, *Essentials of English*

In the spaces provided at the right, indicate the appropriate terminal punctuation for each of the following sentences by writing the word *period* or by writing a question mark (?) or an exclamation mark (!).

EXAMPLES:

They walked down to the store	period
Will you go to the dance with me	?
What a horrible sight it was	!

1. Can you see the tower from here   _____

2. Oh, I can't stand the sight of him   _____

3. Please send me a dozen ripe peaches   _____

4. I asked if I could visit the patient   _____

5. I don't know how many of the delegates will attend the convention _____

6. Help, I'm falling   _____

7. He asked me why I didn't hire more men   _____

8. Do you know that many of the cars on the highways are unsafe both for their drivers and for others on the road   _____

9. Let me ask him to go with us to the seashore   _____

10. What a fool I've been   _____

11. What will the boss say when he discovers that we have mixed up the orders   _____

12. Don't expect to learn to play the game well without devoting a great deal of time to mastering the fundamentals   _____

13. I inquired about the conditions of the roads before setting off on the journey

_____

14. They asked me why my brother had not come with me

_____

15. We can inquire about the mail at the post office

_____

16. Can you tell me how many gallons of water are needed to fill the swimming pool

_____

17. What a marvelous speaker he is

_____

18. To swim or not to swim, that is the question

_____

19. They questioned him about his past and about his plans for the future

_____

20. Oh, how utterly wretched I am

_____

21. Did you realize that many farms in the state are still without electricity, running water, and adequate heating facilities

_____

22. Can you really decide which of the engines is best simply by looking at them

_____

23. How is it that so many people who enjoy both health and prosperity find that they are really not very happy and even confess to being faintly bored a great deal of the time

_____

24. Philosophy can be very discouraging if one is looking for answers to fundamental questions, but it is very satisfying if one is interested in knowing precisely what the fundamental questions are

_____

25. Why do you require more of your helpers than you are willing to do yourself

_____

61 THE COMMA: TO SEPARATE PARTS OF A SERIES

Section 26A, *Essentials of English*

Some of the following sentences contain words, phrases, or clauses in a series which should be separated from each other by commas. Insert commas where they are needed.

EXAMPLE:

Tom Dick and Harry went swimming.

COMMAS INSERTED: Tom, Dick, and Harry went swimming.

1. The pedestrian stepped off the curb looked about uncertainly and slowly crossed the street.

2. They sent for the doctor and fidgeted until he came.

3. James and Fred and Albert are planning to try out for the team.

4. They ate their lunch under a tall pine tree.

5. He brought home some beautiful Spanish shawls.

6. The new novel has a worn-out tiresome threadbare plot.

7. Nobody knows who invented the alphabet the wheel the sidewalk or kissing.

8. She applied for a position at The County Trust Company Johnson's & West's and Danforth & Robbins.

9. I like a man who is honest in his thinking fair in his dealings generous in his charities.

10. Wordsworth Coleridge Keats Shelley and Byron are the most prominent of the Romantic poets.

11. The driver released the brake stepped on the gas and disappeared from sight.

12. Whoever enjoys work knows how to relax and relishes the sheer experience of living has attained the secret of a contented life.

13. The first act of the play was exciting the second act was interesting but the third act was dull.

14. She couldn't decide whether to paint the walls green blue or yellow.

15. Equal pay for equal work abortion on demand and 24-hour day care centers are three major demands of the Women's Liberation Movement.

16. The city was founded in 1642 incorporated as a village in 1800 and chartered as a city in 1905.

17. George Stephenson was an inventor who was born in 1781 and died in 1848.

18. The captain set sail from Albany and piloted his boat down the Hudson River and into the Atlantic.

19. One of the most interesting features of the submarine is its watertight airtight conning tower.

20. Some are born great some achieve greatness and some have greatness thrust upon them.

21. His studies included chemistry and physics and astronomy.

22. The tiresome and unimaginative pattern seemed to be repeated over and over and over.

23. Harriet Tubman escaped from slavery in Maryland made nineteen trips south and freed more than three hundred slaves.

24. Vermont New Hampshire Massachusetts Maine Rhode Island and Connecticut are known as the New England states.

25. He punched kicked scratched and bit everybody who came near him.

62 THE COMMA: TO SEPARATE CLAUSES OF A COMPOUND SENTENCE JOINED BY A COORDINATING CONJUNCTION

Section 26B, *Essentials of English*

Some of the following are compound sentences; others are not. For each sentence which contains independent clauses joined by a coordinating conjunction, write the conjunction in the space to the right, placing the comma in its proper position relative to the conjunction.

EXAMPLES:

He ran quickly to the railroad station and bought a ticket.

He ran quickly to the railroad station and he bought a ticket.

_____

, and _____

1. The organization was supported by voluntary contributions and by donations from the Community Chest and other welfare organizations.

_____

2. The country's economic condition gradually improved during his administration but there were still many people who depended on charity for a living.

_____

3. Canisius established Jesuit centers in many parts of Germany and taught in German universities.

_____

4. The Chinese Empire gradually lost its sovereignty over Tibet for the province was large and very difficult to control.

_____

5. Some temptations come to the industrious but all temptations attack the idle.

_____

6. Leonardo da Vinci attained supremacy in the field of painting and exhibited his love for vivid color in all of his masterpieces.

_____

7. A great tournament was held to celebrate the royal marriage and all but twenty-five of the noblemen in the entire kingdom were present.

_____

8. Caterpillars are regarded by many as loathsome creatures yet butterflies are a delight to all who see them.

_____

9. You can see the eclipse clearly by viewing it through dark glasses or you can get the same effect by holding a piece of overexposed film in front of your eyes.

_____

10. The prisoner was not excited at the prospect of obtaining a parole nor did the opportunity to begin a new life arouse in him any trace of emotion.

11. It is too soon yet to take the things out of the refrigerator for the guests are either late or are not coming at all.

12. The rooms in the house were either too large or too small and the closets were large but poorly arranged.

13. The Athenean council of the Areopagus had a legendary history that indicated that it was a very ancient and highly venerated institution yet its history before Solon was either so little known or so completely ignored that most people in later times believed it to have been founded by him.

14. The belief in ghosts or apparitions has had an immense effect on the religious development of the human race and many early religions had their origin in attempts to propitiate evil spirits or to invoke the assistance of spirits regarded as benign.

15. Buildings made of stone are more permanent than those made of wood for they are not likely to burn up or rot away.

16. Henry Hudson sailed into the Delaware Bay in 1609 but he found the water shallow and so left to later navigators the honor of exploring the yet unknown reaches of the river which flowed into it.

17. Anthropology is known as the science of man and may be regarded as a branch of zoology or the science of animals.

18. The art of diving to considerable depths under water to bring up coral or sponges has been practiced in the Indian seas from very early times and descendants of the earliest divers continue the ancient custom.

19. Daniel Defoe read an account of the shipwreck of Alexander Selkirk and was inspired to write *Robinson Crusoe* because of his admiration for what Selkirk had accomplished on a desert island before he was rescued.

20. Send for the doctor as soon as you can and keep the patient warm until he comes.

63 THE COMMA: TO SEPARATE NON-INTEGRATED SENTENCE ELEMENTS

Section 26C, *Essentials of English*

Each of the following sentences contains a word or phrase which is not an integral part of the structure of the sentence. Indicate in the spaces to the right how these elements should be set off from the basic sentences by writing each comma which should be inserted together with the word which precedes it. If two commas are required, write the words and commas in the order in which they occur in the sentence.

EXAMPLES:

Nevertheless he insisted on coming.

Nevertheless,

It was scarcely too late on the other hand to apply for the position of ticket collector at the theatre.

late,

hand,

1. Dinner being late the guests had plenty of time to get acquainted with each other before entering the dining room.

1. _____

2. Yes I think I can arrange it.

2. _____

3. You don't have to worry about getting dates you lucky girl with your looks and disposition.

3. _____

4. The candidate insisted moreover that he would win the nomination without the backing of any special interests.

4. _____

5. By the way have you seen any good plays lately?

5. _____

6. Nonsense you don't need to take heavy clothes with you when you go on the Mediterranean cruise.

6. _____

7. Bring me a knife and fork Edna so I can eat this fine food without being accused of never having learned good manners.

7. _____

8. The stockholders felt confident the time being ripe that their proposal would be accepted by the board of directors.

8. _____

9. Consequently they went to the meeting in high spirits.

9. _____

10. It seems to me Mr. Hudson that you are embarking on a very dangerous and troublesome undertaking.

10.

11. No I don't see how I can possibly accept the responsibility.

11.

12. It seems obvious things being what they are that we shall have to postpone the meeting indefinitely.

12.

13. See here Doctor exactly how long do you expect me to stay on this ridiculous diet and drink this nauseating tonic?

13.

14. I've waited too long however to give up hope of being entirely cured in the long run.

14.

15. Anyway there is no harm in trying.

15.

16. Well it's high time you got some of the work done.

16.

17. Oh I didn't know you were there.

17.

18. Let me know for goodness' sake when you expect to get your affairs sufficiently organized to be able to leave the city.

18.

19. Mrs. Tomlison I am delighted to make your acquaintance.

19.

20. The sacrifices having been performed and the winds being favorable the Achaeans set sail for Troy.

20.

21. Mr. President I am happy to report that the mission has been satisfactorily accomplished.

21.

22. I'm very sorry to hear you say that Professor.

22.

23. In the first place we don't have enough money to do it even if we really want to.

23.

24. Altogether it seemed like a hopeless undertaking.

24.

25. It was very good of you to come to see me my friends.

25.

64 THE COMMA: TO SET OFF A LONG PHRASE OR CLAUSE PRECEDING THE SUBJECT

Section 26D, *Essentials of English*

In some of the following sentences, a phrase or clause of five words or more precedes the subject and should be set off by a comma. Where such a comma is required, write the last word of the introductory phrase or clause followed by a comma in the space provided.

EXAMPLES:

After many long years of tedious and unrewarding work he felt that he had earned the right to retire.   _____work,_____

After dinner we all went to the movies.   _____

1. When we collected money for the Red Cross and other charitable organizations we felt that we were being useful citizens.   _____

2. In the desk he found copies of old newspapers and magazines.   _____

3. In a rage he stalked out of the office and slammed the door.   _____

4. As he held his cigar between his teeth a puzzled look came into his face.   _____

5. At lunch today I ran into three old friends whom I had not seen for years.   _____

6. If I don't get back to the office in time I shall have to explain why I was delayed.   _____

7. In reply to my lame and halting letter there came a most courteous and encouraging response.   _____

8. After a short stroll along the bank of the river we turned in for the night.   _____

9. As I told you when you insisted on buying that expensive car you act too much on impulse.   _____

10. Only yesterday the news came that the treaty had been ratified.   _____

11. If we can persuade our friends to join us we shall be happy to accept your invitation.   _____

12. At last he realized that there was little he could do to ameliorate the unfortunate situation.

13. For a moment I didn't know whether it was John or his younger brother.

_____

14. Speaking of books I haven't read a really good novel in the last six months.

_____

15. Like his father and his grandfather he had penetrating blue eyes and a square, manly chin.

_____

16. On one occasion the famous private detective found himself completely baffled.

_____

17. In a few years his anger will subside and even the cause of his fury will have been forgotten.

_____

18. By the time we have learned all the intricacies of the new game it will be too late to play it.

_____

19. In Greenwich Village many outstanding writers and artists did their finest work.

_____

20. After the false Armistice Day of November 7th the real peace celebration of November 11th came as an anti-climax.

_____

21. Busy with his painting in the morning and his reading in the afternoon he found no time to be bored.

_____

22. To my dying day I shall never forget the look on her face when I asked her if she would like to go to Africa.

_____

23. For many years the cyclical theory of history fascinated professional historians and laymen alike.

_____

24. In a little room at the back of the store he kept the few valuable objects that he possessed.

_____

25. When the elected representatives of a society make a decision all the members of that society are bound by it.

_____

65 THE COMMA: TO INDICATE INTERRUPTIONS OF NORMAL WORD ORDER

Section 26E, *Essentials of English*

Most, but not all, of the following sentences contain words, phrases, or clauses which interrupt the natural flow of thought and should be set off by commas. In the spaces provided at the right, indicate the proper placing of such commas as are required by writing each comma and the word preceding it in the order in which the commas should appear in the sentence.

EXAMPLES:

I certainly expected to see you there.

I intended as I told you to be present at the reception which was held at the auditorium last Wednesday night.

intended,

you,

1. The tribute it seemed clear could not be paid in full or even in part without destroying the economy of the country.

1. _____

2. He found a trunk full of old clothes dirty and moth-eaten stored away in the far corner of the storage room in the basement.

2. _____

3. You will I am sure want to make up your own mind on this question since you are the one most affected.

3. _____

4. Ninety percent of our graduates as you know find employment within six months of graduation.

4. _____

5. They managed to decide on a name Christine for the yacht by writing all the suggestions on slips of paper and drawing one from a hat.

5. _____

6. The two men walked down the road together while Thomas the tall one talked incessantly about his plans.

6. _____

7. The members of congress most of them worried about re-election try to avoid taking positions that will offend their constituents.

7. _____

8. It was tempting he discovered to caution others against making the kind of mistake that had ruined his own career.

8. _____

9. She would always remember that month April as the high point of her business career.

9. _____

10. He could not believe that his secretary usually very reliable would be late without a good reason.

10. _____

11. The firm was indeed fortunate to secure the services of such an outstanding electrical engineer.

11. _____

12. It was after a particularly trying winter of arduous duties that Eleanor footloose and fancy-free got in her car and drove west.

12. _____

13. There seemed little reason to doubt that John being what he was would find any difficulty in attaining his goal.

13. _____

14. They visited a castle that larger than some and older than most gave them considerable insight into medieval life.

14. _____

15. It was a French philosopher Montaigne who said that the course of education was from ignorance to knowledge and from knowledge to the discovery of one's own ignorance.

15. _____

16. They named her Eleanor after her mother and her mother's favorite cousin who had been killed in an accident.

16. _____

17. It was in the year 1066 that the Normans successfully invaded and conquered England.

17. _____

18. He stood there listening to the gentle lapping of the waves on the shore the only sound to be heard and began to relax.

18. _____

19. It will take a long time as I told you to draw up plans for the kind of building you insist on having.

19. _____

20. It is the secretary's responsibility his main responsibility to send out notices to the members.

20. _____

66 THE COMMA: TO SET OFF NONRESTRICTIVE ELEMENTS

Section 26F, *Essentials of English*

Some of the following sentences contain nonrestrictive words, phrases, or clauses. Wherever such non-essential elements appear, indicate the correct punctuation by writing the comma and the word preceding it in the space to the right. If two commas are required, indicate them in the order in which they should appear in the sentence.

EXAMPLES:

He was very fond of his father as boys usually are.	father,
He was the tallest of all the doctors who travelled to Chicago to attend the convention.	
His father who was an unusually tall and distinguished-looking man was a leading citizen in the community.	father, man,

1. He spends hours listening to the troubles of the people who come to him for assistance or advice.

    1. _____

2. He devotes a great deal of his time listening to the troubles of his patients who come from near and far.

    2. _____

3. The student who submitted the paper on cartels will be asked to represent the college at the meeting of The Economics Society.

    3. _____

4. Any student who can write a good article on cartels should be encouraged to major in economics.

    4. _____

5. John Frazer who wrote a good paper on cartels was encouraged by his professors to major in economics.

    5. _____

6. Robert Frost the celebrated American poet lectured to large and appreciative audiences all over the country.

    6. _____

7. The poet Robert Frost lectured to large and appreciative audiences and sometimes read from his own works.

    7. _____

8. The word *derrick* is derived from the name of a celebrated British hangman of the seventeenth century.

8. _____

9. He spent the evening playing rummy with his friend John Glade who works in the same plant.

9. _____

10. He spent the evening playing cards with a group of men who work in the same plant.

10. _____

11. Some words like *maverick* and *martinet* are derived from the names of people who became famous for particular personality traits.

11. _____

12. The train I am waiting for is the express that gets to San Francisco before noon.

12. _____

13. The San Francisco Express the train I am waiting for is already twenty minutes late.

13. _____

14. A play like *Hamlet* cannot be fully appreciated or even completely understood by people who read it hastily.

14. _____

15. Many plays like *Hamlet* were written for a reading public as well as for a theatre audience.

15. _____

16. He often thought fondly of the city where he had spent the major part of his early life.

16. _____

17. He often thought fondly of New Orleans where he had spent the major part of his early life.

17. _____

18. O'Neill's play *Anna Christie* is much more conventional in form than most of his other dramas.

18. _____

19. The roads that were paved with macadam have remained smoother than those paved with brick.

19. _____

20. Virgil's only long poem *The Aeneid* was deliberately written to celebrate the reign of Caesar Augustus and glorify the Roman Empire.

20. _____

67 THE COMMA: TO EMPHASIZE CONTRAST AND TO PREVENT MISREADING

Sections 26G, 26H, *Essentials of English*

Each of the following sentences can be improved by the insertion of a comma to eliminate confusion caused by misreading or to set off contrasted sentence elements. Indicate where the comma should be placed in each sentence by writing the comma and the word preceding it in the space to the right.

EXAMPLES:

He was willing to pay but not that much.   pay,

During the winter days become shorter.   winter,

1. Although hard to find uranium is worth more than its weight in gold.   _____

2. They hunted all over the town and all over the county and all over the state and found nothing.   _____

3. She was always happy never sad.   _____

4. Since the gymnasium was intended for adults only children were not permitted to play in it.   _____

5. Beneath the cellar was lined with shelves full of jellies and jams.   _____

6. They expected to meet Jim not his brother.   _____

7. Turning around the dog changed its position and lay down again.   _____

8. The engineers are certain that they will complete the project but not for a long time.   _____

9. He was the kind of person who worked for pleasure not money.   _____

10. After all the rewards of professional enterprise are not exclusively financial.   _____

11. The medicine was good for the doctor knew I wouldn't take anything that tasted bitter.   _____

12. Whenever he pitched the ball was almost certain to go right across the plate.

_____

13. I was willing to try it once but never again.

_____

14. In dealing with children who can tell in advance what their moods and reactions are likely to be?

_____

15. Working with the company salesmen find it to their advantage to keep precise records of all their calls.

_____

16. It hasn't rained yet the ground is wet.

_____

17. He will eat when he wants to not before.

_____

18. It was hard work that accounted for his success not luck.

_____

19. Not expecting him to do the job over his boss was pleased that he had been so conscientious.

_____

20. In fancy old recollections take on qualities of glamour and charm which the originals never possessed.

_____

21. Having met the two families found themselves more congenial than they had anticipated.

_____

22. The cost of living goes steadily up seldom down.

_____

23. During the year 1943 automobiles were involved in accidents in the state; 173 of this number were fatal.

_____

24. After they had sung the quartet were assigned to their places of honor on the dais.

_____

25. The president not the congress is responsible for the conduct of foreign affairs.

_____

68 REVIEW: THE COMMA

Section 26, *Essentials of English*

Insert commas in the following article wherever they are needed. Then list them in the spaces to the right in the order in which they occur, identifying each comma by writing the word immediately preceding it.

Although few Americans ever stop to think about it, there is mystery in our conversation, in the everyday phrases that come so easily to our tongues. The literal meaning may have been long forgotten but the phrases remain in our language like fossils reminding us vaguely of another era. What is the original meaning for example of *apple of one's eye one fell swoop brown as a berry armed to the teeth* or *bite off more than one can chew?*

Many a grandparent has looked proudly at an offspring of his family tree and referred to the infant as *the apple of my eye.* But why *apple?* And why *apple of my eye?* In early days the pupil of the eye was thought to be perfectly round and spherical. In that unscientific time the best way to describe the pupil was to compare it to a common object like an apple and so the pupil came to be known as the *apple of the eye.* The obvious meaning of the Biblical verse: "Keep me as the apple of the eye" (Psalms 17:8) is "protect me and keep me as if I were as valuable as the pupil of the eye." An even earlier use of the term is found in Deuteronomy 32:10: "He led him about he instructed him and he kept him as the apple of his eye." Nowadays not even an optometrist looking proudly at his first-born would be aware of what he really means when he says: *That's the apple of my eye.*

it,
conversation,
1.
2.
3.
4.
5.
6.
7.
8.
9.
10.
11.
12.
13.
14.
15.
16.
17.
18.
19.
20.

Has there ever been a summer at the beach when someone   21. _____

failed to use the old cliché: *You're as brown as a berry?*   22. _____

Yet who has ever seen a brown berry? We have blackberries   23. _____

red raspberries blueberries and berries of many another hue   24. _____

but none that is brown. Some scholars in trying to account   25. _____

for the phrase have suggested that the coffee bean may be   26. _____

the intended berry. The phrase was used by the poet Chaucer   27. _____

however over two hundred years before coffee was known in   28. _____

England. Chaucer in his quaint Middle English spelling used   29. _____

the phrase to describe a horse which was *as broun as a berye.*   30. _____

This is still another mystery that has survived even in an   31. _____

era of sun lamps and quick-tanning lotions. No matter what   32. _____

the method one can still become unaccountably *brown as a*   33. _____

berry. In any event this is more appropriate is it not than   34. _____

being as purple as a mulberry blue as a blueberry or as char-   35. _____

treuse as a grape?

69 THE SEMICOLON

Section 28, *Essentials of English*

The following sentences are punctuated internally only by commas. In some of these sentences, the punctuation is correct. In others the commas should be replaced by semicolons. In still others one or more of the commas should be replaced by semicolons to assist the reader. Wherever you think that a semicolon should be used, write the semicolon in the space provided together with the word that precedes it. If more than one semicolon should be inserted in a sentence, indicate your insertions by listing them in the order in which they appear in the sentence.

EXAMPLES:

He took enough provisions to last him for several days, for he didn't know how long the journey would take.

Mother looked all over to find an appropriate birthday present, she finally discovered exactly what she wanted.   present;

They sowed beans, peas, and corn in one field, oats,   field;
wheat, and barley in another, and lettuce, carrots, cab-   another;
bage, beets, radishes, spinach, cauliflower, and swiss
chard in the third.

1. It was the first anniversary of their arrival in Chicago, and   1. _____
both of them wanted to celebrate it.

2. Here am I, little Jumping Joan, when nobody's with me, I'm   2. _____
all alone.

3. The temple is in length, within the walls, five yards and two   3. _____
feet, in breadth, two yards and a few inches.

4. He was a man of good sense, moreover, he had benefited by   4. _____
extensive travel and the acquaintance of many talented persons.

5. We had hoped to make the journey on foot, however, the bad   5. _____
weather prevented us from carrying out this ambitious project.

6. There was an old woman who lived on a hill, if she isn't gone, she lives there still.

6. _____

7. I begged the guests not to discuss politics, I was anxious to avoid an argument.

7. _____

8. I cannot trust my own judgment, therefore, I always take a friend with me when I go shopping.

8. _____

9. The premier spoke for about two hours in defense of his policy, he assured the people that it was the most effective method for ensuring peace.

9. _____

10. There were five hits, two runs, no errors in the first inning, two hits, no runs, one error in the second, no hits, no runs, no errors in the third.

10. _____

70 THE COLON,
THE DASH, THE HYPHEN

Sections 29, 30, 31, *Essentials of English*

The following sentences are punctuated internally only by commas. Wherever you think that a colon or a dash should be supplied or should be substituted for a comma, write the colon or dash and the word preceding it in the space provided. If two or more punctuation marks should be inserted in a single sentence, indicate these insertions by listing them in the order in which they occur in the sentence.

EXAMPLES:

People want and need one thing above all others, leadership.　　　　others:
_____

Among the guests were the Flynns, the Westcotes, and the
Grants.
_____

I explained at great length, I didn't realize what I was saying,　　length—
that I had no previous acquaintance with the suspect.　　　　　　saying—
_____

1. The following instruments were ordered for the band, three trombones,　　1. _____
three trumpets, one sousaphone, four snare drums, one bass drum, two
French horns, and one pair of cymbals.　　_____

_____

2. Nearly all of the men in the lodge, the women weren't invited, at-　　2. _____
tended the convention at Chicago last year.

_____

3. Unable to hide his confusion, "I, you, we both should take some of the　　3. _____
blame," he gulped.

_____

4. The tickets were distributed as follows, forty to the freshmen, sixty to　　4. _____
the sophomores, eighty to the juniors, and one hundred to the seniors.

_____

5. When all is said and done, there was only one person who loved him,　　5. _____
his mother.

_____

6. Among those present were the mayor and two of the councilmen.   6. _____

7. She struggled all her life to be prominent in Society, she attained her goal.   7. _____

   _____

8. The members of the sales force were assigned to cover ten different states, Wyoming, Nebraska, Oklahoma, Michigan, Illinois, Ohio, Pennsylvania, Kansas, Montana, Arkansas.   8. _____

   _____

   _____

9. Spread out on the table were pencils, paper, and erasers.   9. _____

10. My first assignment, it couldn't have been better, was to photograph Aztec ruins in remote parts of Mexico.   10. _____

    _____

In some of the following phrases, hyphens should be inserted. In the spaces at the right, indicate the correct use of the hyphen by rewriting any part of the phrase that should be hyphenated.

EXAMPLE:

The Tilton Edwards fight   Tilton-Edwards

11. to reecho the sound   _____

12. a yellow green dress   _____

13. a pretty pink dress   _____

14. impossible to recreate the world   _____

15. a lighter than air aircraft   _____

16. the Yale Harvard game   _____

17. a dyed in the wool conservative   _____

18. twenty three books   _____

19. a large, well lighted room   _____

20. an antiintellectual   _____

71 QUOTATION MARKS

Sections 34A, 34B, 34C, 34D, *Essentials of English*

The following sentences include direct **and indirect** quotations and titles of short pieces. Indicate the correct use of quotation marks and other accompanying punctuation by writing the first and last words of the quotation together with the correct punctuation in the spaces at the right.

EXAMPLES:

He said that he didn't care.

I have no intention of going to the concert next
Friday, he said in a surly tone of voice.

	"I
	Friday,"

If the president is sick, who will preside at the meeting? asked the secretary of The Men's Club.

	"If
	meeting?"

1. It will be necessary for us to raise additional funds to meet
our current expenses, according to the treasurer's report.

1. _____

2. The treasurer reported it will be necessary for us to raise additional funds to meet current expenses.

2. _____

3. That taking an active part in local politics is none of our
business and was never intended to be a function of this
organization, he said, is obvious to anybody who has taken
the time and trouble to study our constitution carefully.

3. _____

4. The exact words of the judge when pronouncing sentence
were hanged by the neck until dead.

4. _____

5. After dinner he read a short poem of his own composition
entitled The Riverboat on the Mississippi.

5. _____

6. Mr. Davenport asked me if I would be willing to accept the

6. _____

money in exchange for a partnership in my firm, The Excello Zipper Co.

_____

_____

7. The sergeant was very angry with the two members of the patrol who had become separated from the others. Didn't you hear the captain say, Keep together no matter what happens? he shouted.

7. _____

_____

_____

_____

8. After consuming a hearty and leisurely breakfast in the dining room of The Robert Smith Hotel, he got to work on his short story The Friend of the People; he managed to finish it before noon.

8. _____

_____

_____

9. Will the audience kindly stand and sing the first and last stanzas of America? the master of ceremonies asked, concluding the celebration on a patriotic note which was so unusual as to arouse comment.

9. _____

_____

_____

10. I can't find my thimble. Has anybody seen it? asked Mother after she had rummaged through her sewing basket without success.

10. _____

_____

11. I enjoyed reading every page of the book. I was especially delighted by the chapter entitled What About the Future? he replied in answer to my question.

11. _____

_____

_____

12. It is useless, he said, to inquire about the exact dates of events in the remote past, for the actual records of these occurrances were recorded only in the memories of the people who witnessed them.

12. _____

_____

_____

_____

_____

13. Pull your chair over so you will be close to the fire, she said. Are you so warm-blooded that you don't mind the cold on a night like this, or are you so cold-blooded that you prefer to sit at a distance from your friends?

13. _____
_____
_____
_____

14. The article in the magazine that particularly attracted my attention was What Does Anyone Really Know? said my aunt who was notorious all over the neighborhood for always being sure about everything.

14. _____
_____
_____
_____

15. We were very anxious to hear about his trip, but he said that he was in no mood to say anything about it. It's just something that I don't want to talk about—now or at any time in the future, he insisted.

15. _____
_____
_____
_____

16. No matter what we asked her to sing, her response was always that she didn't remember the words. John finally became annoyed. Can you sing Home Sweet Home? he asked in a tone of utter disgust.

16. _____
_____
_____
_____

17. He had already swum more than fifty yards away from the boat when we heard his anguished cry for help. Save me! he shouted.

17. _____
_____
_____
_____

18. She told the others that she would be ready to leave by ten o'clock, but when they called for her she greeted them by saying that she had changed her mind and wasn't going at all.

18. _____
_____
_____
_____

19. What he actually said was I don't like it very much: we didn't press him for a fuller explanation.

19. _____

_____

20. Don't let me ever again catch you saying, I'm stupid! John's mother screamed at him when he quietly murmured those fatal words as an excuse for the low grades on his report card.

20. _____

_____

_____

72 ITALICS AND QUOTATION MARKS TO INDICATE TITLES

Sections 34A, and 35A, *Essentials of English*

Underline or enclose in quotation marks any words in the following sentences which require such treatment. Be sure to distinguish between titles that should be italicized (underlined) and those which should be placed in quotation marks.

EXAMPLES:

He read Johnny's First Christmas in The Youth's Companion.

CORRECTED: He read "Johnny's First Christmas" in <u>The Youth's Companion</u>.

1. Have you ever read Tolstoy's novel War and Peace?

2. He chose his text from a passage in the tenth chapter of Deuteronomy.

3. He subscribed to the London Times for twenty years.

4. The article Take Care of Your Heart was reprinted by permission of the magazine.

5. Poe said that he wrote The Raven in accordance with his theory that poems should be brief.

6. The original manuscript of Shelley's Ode to the West Wind covered four pages.

7. He studied at Blair Academy.

8. Wagner's opera Lohengrin was performed at The Metropolitan Opera House.

9. Jonathan Edwards was very fond of quoting from the Bible.

10. One of the most widely-read magazines in America was The Literary Digest.

11. A regular department in the magazine was called The Lexicographer's Easy Chair.

12. Have you read the editorial Changing Conditions in yesterday's paper?

13. Sheridan's play The School for Scandal was originally presented at the Theatre Royal in Drury Lane.

14. Vergil's Aeneid is a long epic poem.

15. He first saw the poem in Ward's anthology The English Poets.

16. The Tower of Pisa is one of the strangest sights in Italy.

17. They sang the first stanza of The Star-Spangled Banner.

18. The minister's sermon Twenty Years from Now made the congregation thoughtful.

19. Fielding's novel Tom Jones is a triumph of realism and humor.

20. His book was printed at The Oxford Press.

21. He read his article at The Literary Club.

22. Samuel Johnson wrote the first great English dictionary.

23. Mencken and Nathan made fun of American stupidity every month in their magazine in a section labelled Americana.

24. Gone With the Wind was a four-hour motion picture.

25. A Dissertation upon Roast Pig is Lamb's most famous essay.

73 PUNCTUATION: REVIEW (1)

Sections 25, 26, 27, 28, 29, 30, 31, 34, 35, *Essentials of English*

Punctuate the following exercises, adding all needed punctuation, including quotation marks and italics.

EXAMPLE:

John my oldest brother said that he had read Shakespeare's Othello with great pleasure It taught me a lot about jealousy he said

PUNCTUATED: John, my oldest brother, said that he had read Shakespeare's Othello with great pleasure. "It taught me a lot about jealousy," he said.

1. He took his club in his hand and with it he struck a stag such a great blow that he brayed vehemently and at his braying the animals came flocking as numerous as the stars in the sky so rapidly that before I could ask What are you doing that for the glade was packed solid with woodland creatures

2. There were openings for five stenographers two typists and four filing clerks in the shipping department three secretaries six copywriters and four layout men in the advertising department and two accountants and five bookkeepers in the controller's office

3. John Miles sent his short story The Open Door to The Little Magazine Devil take them he raged when it was rejected I'll bet he added wryly the editor would have rejected The Outcasts of Poker Flat if he had never heard of Bret Harte as a famous writer of short stories

4. To Whom It May Concern This is to certify that Mary Smith has been employed by this firm for the past ten years and has always been efficient cooperative and diligent in every way

5. This is an unlooked for and unhoped for honor my friends said my uncle when he was given a party in honor of his eighty first birthday Anyone who has lived as long as I have he continued is lucky to have any friends left and I am sure we all ask ourselves How many more years shall we be among the living

6. The following committee members were present at the meeting Edward Jones Frank Simmons Anna Metcalf Leslie Hall and Janet Fox

7. After a long hot dusty ride on what must have been the oldest daycoach on the railroad my friend Bob finally exploded Never again he roared John if you ever ask me and I mean it to go anywhere with you again see to it that you pick a cool day and a pleasanter means of transportation

8. On a never to be forgotten day in early August we arrived in Mexico City The weather was perfect the hotel reservation was paid for and we were ready to enjoy the first real vacation we had had in twenty three years

9. Ernest Hemingway the celebrated American author took his title for his novel The Sun Also Rises from the Biblical book of Ecclesiastes The title is effective in itself however it is more meaningful if one is aware of the entire passage from which it was taken not to mention the generally pessimistic and gloomy outlook conveyed by the entire book

10. The rains having come early we anticipated an excellent crop that year furthermore we had plowed deeply fertilized well and sowed the finest seed

74 PUNCTUATION: REVIEW (2)

Sections 25, 26, 27, 28, 29, 30, 31, 34, 35, *Essentials of English*

Punctuate the following exercises, adding all needed punctuation, including quotation marks and italics.

EXAMPLE:

John my oldest brother said that he had read Shakespeare's Othello with great pleasure It taught me a lot about jealousy he said

PUNCTUATED: John, my oldest brother, said that he had read Shakespeare's Othello with great pleasure. "It taught me a lot about jealousy," he said.

1. When my uncle took his family on a summer vacation in Maine he complained about the weather the prices and the food When he took his family on a winter vacation in Florida he complained about the weather the prices and the food My aunt plans to take a vacation by herself next year

2. At the world famous battle of Marathon the disposition of the Greek forces was as follows the right wing was led by Callimachus the center was divided among the other leaders of the Athenians and the left wing was formed by the Plataeans When the Persians advanced in full battle array the Athenians in the center charged them at full speed The Persians thought that the Greeks were out of their minds for they saw a mere handful of men coming at them While this small force was engaging the Persians however the two Greek wings converged upon the center fought the enemy valiantly and completely routed them

3. In his essay On Flattery one of the thirty character sketches that make up the work known as The Moral Characters Theophrastus states Flattery is a base manner of conversation that tends only to the advantage of the flatterer He goes on to describe the many things a flatterer does to make himself agreeable to everybody he meets He concludes by saying In short the flatterer has but one design in all his words and actions and that is to catch men by their weak side and to ingratiate himself into their favor

4. John and Mary were driving down a long narrow bumpy country road on the way to visit John's cousin Will you try to like her said John She is a very easy to get along with kind of person

How old is she asked Mary

She must be let's see why she must be twenty one by now How time flies It seems only yesterday that she was a little girl in pigtails reciting Mary Mary Quite Contrary and singing I'll never forget it The Farmer in the Dell in a funny high squeaky baby voice

5. The men who came to Independence Hall to volunteer their services were angry when they were informed that they were not needed although there was really no reason for them to be annoyed

6. I see by The New York Times said Mother that the prices keep right on going up Don't tell father He will only say Don't you know that prices go only one way up

7. The room was furnished handsomely not elaborately moreover everything about it bespoke the exquisite taste of the owner

8. The old oak tree gnarled and majestic dominated the lawn other trees seemed puny by comparison

75 WRITING PARAGRAPHS

Section 36, *Essentials of English*

In the space provided below and on the back of this page, write two paragraphs beginning with any two of the topic sentences that follow. Use the order of arrangement that is suggested for each topic sentence.

1. From the first to the third grade, my experiences with the opposite sex were innocent and uninhibited. (Time Order)

2. The best way to describe Picasso's painting *Guernica* is to go from left to right on his canvas. (Space Order)

3. In evaluating my use of time, I like to list everything I do in a day in a rank of ascending importance. (Order of Climax)

4. The best way to explain the law of pneumatics is to show how the brakes work on an automobile. (From the Familiar to the Unfamiliar)

5. Thurman Munson was valuable to the New York Yankees in a great many ways. (From the General to the Particular)

76 DEVELOPING PARAGRAPHS

Section 36B, *Essentials of English*

In the space provided below and on the back of this page, write two paragraphs beginning with any two of the topic sentences that follow. Use the method of development that is suggested for each topic sentence.

1. My bedroom is a reflection of my personality. (Particulars and Details)

2. Changing a tire on a bicycle is an operation that must be carried out in a precise series of steps. (Logical Divisions—Steps in a Process)

3. Professional sports and high school athletics are different in many ways and similar in only a few points. (Comparison and Contrast)

4. The beginning of one's education in the first grade is like starting a journey. (Analogy)

5. A funny thing happened to me on the way to class today. (Narration)

6. When people are idle, bored, or frustrated, trouble often develops. (Cause and Effect)

7. Courage can have many different aspects in various situations. (Instances and Examples)

8. What is freedom? (Definition)

9. A museum of natural history has many interesting things to delight the eye and stimulate the mind. (Particulars and Details)

10. The old man who sells papers near the subway entrance is interesting both in his mannerisms and his dress. (Description)

77 USING TRANSITIONAL EXPRESSIONS FOR PARAGRAPH COHERENCE

Section 36F, *Essentials of English*

Underline the transitional expressions used in the following paragraph. Identify the type of each transitional expression (addition, contrast, comparison, etc.) in the blank adjacent to each sentence. Since this is written as an exercise, transitional expressions are used to an excess. This is, therefore, not a model of good style.

No one can exist in this world entirely alone, *however,*	contrast
independent of all other human beings. In fact, one cannot	1.
go through a day without, indeed, depending on thousands of	2
others to provide, for instance, our daily necessities of	3.
food and transportation. For this purpose, many persons have	4.
labored to grow or manufacture what we must have, after all,	5.
to carry on even the most basic activities of life. However,	6.
we depend likewise on others for those things that are im-	7.
portant, but not necessities, for example, love, pleasure,	8.
and understanding. Nevertheless, there are some times in our	9.
lives when we need, it is true, to be alone, to have space	10.
around us so that we are free to be ourselves. Consequently,	11.
we treasure our quiet times of solitude; indeed, we count	12.
those times among our greatest benefits. Furthermore, we use	13.
these times of being alone, accordingly, for listening	14.
to the sounds of nature and similarly listening to the deep	15.
thoughts of our innermost selves. For this purpose, we must	16.
avoid the distractions of the busy world. Moreover, we can	17.
only get in touch with our most secret selves, finally,	18.
through that comfortable state of being alone and, in fact,	19.
secure from the judgments of others. At the same time, we	20.

do not want to forget our need for relationships with other

human beings. To sum up, we must realize the importance of

being both social and private persons. When we have reached

our goal of a balance between being a whole person, yet a

person who accepts comfortably, on the other hand, depen-

dence on others, we will have happiness.

21. _____

22. _____

23. _____

24. _____

25. _____

26. _____

78 MAKING PARAGRAPHS COHERENT

Section 36F, *Essentials of English*

The following paragraph contains a topic sentence as its first sentence, but the remaining sentences are not placed in any logical order. The sentences are all of the same pattern, and there are no transitional words or phrases to make this collection of words into an orderly, coherent paragraph. Write your version in the space provided on the back of this page.

There are many things that have to be done in order to plan a successful vacation trip to Europe. Find the least expensive round-trip flights. Purchase these tickets ahead of time. Reserve rooms in centrally located, moderately priced hotels or guest houses. Buy a book that lists accommodations and good sight-seeing areas. Get a book that has the basic foreign language phrases you will need, and practice saying them. Learn about the Eurail pass and determine from maps showing your itinerary whether or not the pass will be better than buying each separate railway ticket. Decide where you want to go, and how long you will stay in each place. Read travel books so that you know where to go to get the maximum value from your trip. Learn what months are best for good weather. Rainy days and cold weather can ruin a vacation trip. Learn something about the history of the countries so that what you see will be meaningful. Pack carefully and take as little luggage as possible. Decide when you are going.

79 LIMITING THE SUBJECT

Section 37D, *Essentials of English*

In the space provided below each of the following subjects for an essay, write a more limited title to suggest a more narrowly defined subject. In the space at the right, list the method of limitation.

EXAMPLE:
The Mammals of North America
Squirrels in My Neighborhood _____place_____

1. The Roles of Males and Females: Cave Man to Modern Man

_____

2. What Is Honesty?

_____

3. Why There Are Famines

_____

4. The Executive Branch of Government

_____

5. The Forward Pass as an Offensive Weapon

_____

6. Why Storms Occur

_____

7. What Is Truth?

_____

8. Wedding Customs Throughout the World

_____

9. Wars in the Nineteenth Century

_____

10. Chairing a Committee

_____

80 DETERMINING THE FUNDAMENTAL PURPOSE

Section 38, *Essentials of English*

Choose three of the topic sentences in Exercise 76, and then write two statements of purpose that might be used with these subjects. Use the space below and on the back of the page.

EXAMPLE:
Professional sports and high school athletics are different in many ways and similar in only a few points.

Purpose Statement One: I am writing this essay to show that professional sports, because the quality of performance is so high, are much superior to high school athletics.

Purpose Statement Two: I am writing this essay to show that high school athletics, because they are played for the love of the sport and not for financial reasons, are much superior to professional sports.

81 PLANNING YOUR WRITING

Sections 39 and 40, *Essentials of English*

Choose one of the topics in Exercise 79, and prepare an outline, using the steps suggested in *Essentials of English:* 1. decide on a limited subject, 2. decide on a purpose, 3. write down a list of ideas, 4. eliminate irrelevant items, and 5. organize remaining items into an outline. Write in the space below and on the back of the page.

82 STANDARD ABBREVIATIONS

Section 49E, *Essentials of English*

In the spaces provided write the standard abbreviation for each of the following:

1. *anonymous* _____

2. *books* _____

3. *around* or *about* (as in *"around 1900"*) _____

4. *Chapter 4* _____

5. *Column 2* _____

6. *edited by* _____

7. *for example* _____

8. *and others* _____

9. *Page 19 and the following page* _____

10. *Page 19 and the following pages* _____

11. *the same* _____

12. *that is* (fuller explanation) _____

13. *lines* (as in *Lines 11–12*) _____

14. *manuscript* _____

15. *in the place cited* _____

16. *note well* _____

17. *no date* (of publication) _____

18. *no place* (of publication) _____

19. *pages* (as in *Pages 18–20*) _____

20. *paragraph* (as in *Paragraph 3*) _____

21. *here and there* (materials found throughout a work) _____

22. *so* (usually placed in brackets) _____

23. *translated by* _____

24. *namely* (to introduce a list) _____

25. *volume* (as in *Volume 5*) _____

83 FOOTNOTE TECHNIQUES

Sections 49C, 49D, 49E, *Essentials of English*

Fictitious references for footnotes to a fictitious research paper are given below in the order in which they should be presented. Using the customary forms, write each of these footnotes in the spaces provided as if you were preparing an actual paper.

EXAMPLE:

1. Page 47 in a book by John Welsh entitled *Insect Lore,* published in New York City by John Harmon & Co. in 1940.

1. John Welsh, *Insect Lore* (New York: John Harmon & Co., 1940), p. 47.

2. Page 42 in the same book.

2. Ibid., p. 42.

1. Pages 47 to 49 in the second volume of a work entitled *Myths of the Orient* by James Nelson, published in Chicago in 1848 by Norris, Page, & Smith.

1. _____

_____

2. Page 216 of an article written by Sanford Wallis entitled "Trade and Manufacturing" in a book edited by Russell Ford called *Dominant Aspects of the American Economy in the Nineteenth Century*, published by Grant & Norcross in 1900 in Boston.

2. _____

_____

_____

3. Pages 7 to 12 of a book entitled *Paris* written by Jean Reynard and translated into English by Lester Kirk, published by James Hyman in London. No date of publication appears in this volume.

3. _____

_____

4. Page 217 of the book described in Footnote 3.

4. _____

5. A newspaper article entitled "Is Cotton Still King?" signed by Joshua Small. The article appeared in the New Orleans *Bugle* on October 17, 1903 on the second page of the first section.

5. _____

6. A second reference to the article described in Footnote 5.

6. _____

7. Page 67 of a magazine article entitled "Trends and Tendencies in Advertising" written by Victor Harris and Frank Stallman and published in the April, 1940 issue of a magazine called *Selling*.

7. _____

_____

8. Page 119 of Jean Reynard's *Paris*, described in Footnote 3.

8. _____

9. Pages 74 to 79 of a book written by J. Miles Prendergast entitled *Dukes and Dutchesses*. (The word *Dutchesses* is misspelled in the title of the book.) There is no indication in the book of when or where it was published.

9. _____

10. An article on John Bunyan in the eleventh edition of the *Encyclopaedia Brittannica*. It occurs on page 94 of the third volume.

10. _____

_____

84 FOOTNOTE AND BIBLIOGRAPHY TECHNIQUES (Directions)

Sections 49C, 49D, 49E, 49F, 49G, *Essentials of English*

Fictitious references for footnotes for a fictitious research paper are given below. From the materials given, write the footnotes in the same order in the spaces provided on p. 171. Then add a bibliography in proper form and order on p. 172.

1. Page 14 of a short story by Clifford Matthews whicn appeared in an anthology edited by Searle Weeks and Mary Page in 1940. The anthology was entitled *Tales of the Sea*. It was published in Dublin by John O'Neill. The short story was called "Louise."

2. Pages 19 to 21 of the second volume of a three-volume work entitled *Ships of His Majesty's Navy* written by Sir Richard Falkland, published in London in 1860 by the firm of Nelson Briscoe.

3. Page 217 of the first volume of the work described in Footnote 2.

4. Another reference to Page 217 of the first volume of the work described in Footnote 2.

5. Page 127 of a work called *Complete Shipping Guide*. No author or editor is given. It was published in San Francisco by Stuart, Ross, & Co. in 1918.

6. Page 17 of Clifford Matthews' story *Louise*, described in Footnote 1.

7. Page 24 of an article written by Johann Baumgartner and Heinrich Zeller entitled (in translation) "Viking Ship Construction." This article is in a collection of articles on ship construction entitled *Master Builders of the Sea*. The article was translated into English by Edna Morse. The collection was edited by Francis Wilmot and Nelson Parker. It was copyrighted in 1903. No publisher or place of publication is given.

8. Page 110 of a book by Sir Richard Falkland entitled *Sea Fortresses*. The firm of Lindsay Heath published this book in London in 1865.

9. A very specific reference to the seventeenth line of a poem by Margot Sanders entitled "Irridescence." The poem was published in the spring edition (Volume 17, Number 2) of a quarterly entitled *Sand and Spray* in 1916.

10. Lines 27 to 29 of the same poem (described in Footnote 9).

84 FOOTNOTE AND BIBLIOGRAPHY TECHNIQUES (Practice)

Sections 49C, 49D, 49E, 49F, 49G, *Essentials of English*

FOOTNOTES

_____

_____

_____

_____

_____

_____

_____

_____

_____

_____

_____

_____

_____

_____

_____

_____

_____

_____

_____

_____

84 FOOTNOTE AND BIBLIOGRAPHY TECHNIQUES (Practice)

Sections 49C, 49D, 49E, 49F, 49G, *Essentials of English*

BIBLIOGRAPHY

_____

_____

_____

_____

_____

_____

_____

_____

_____

_____

_____

_____

_____

_____

_____

_____

_____

_____

_____

_____

_____

_____

_____

_____

85 CORRECTING MISUSED WORDS AND PHRASES

"Glossary of Words and Phrases Frequently Misused"
Essentials of English

Each of the following sentences contains one misused word or phrase. Enclose the misused word or phrase in parentheses, and write your correction in the space to the right.

EXAMPLE: CORRECTION

The loss of his job had a bad (affect) on his nerves.   effect

1. Since the last paragraph of the contract is not clear to anybody, both parties to the agreement had ought to agree to except it.

2. That kind of a person is such an enemy to society that he should be hanged.

3. I council you to rest and lie quietly in bed until you feel ready to get up.

4. He insisted that he had been led unwillingly to the altar by the women who is now his wife.

5. Anybody who's circumstances have been adverse can sympathize with the misfortunes of others.

6. The tutor found a unusual way to teach the children their lessons.

7. Once the hecklers had been ejected, the town board preceded with the rest of the meeting.

8. John don't know whether the food he eats is healthful or not.

9. The reason for his adverse circumstances, he implied, was because he was born unlucky.

10. Her cold was aggravated by the rainy weather, but when the sun came out, she felt alright.

11. Less people than ever are willing to invest all their principal in stock.

12. Therefor, it seems sensible to infer that no large rise in the stock market is to be expected.

13. I am afraid that its too late to avert the catastrophe which threatens us.

14. I myself have been affected in my attitude toward life by a great amount of people.

15. The principle of the school is proud of being an alumnus of the school because of its excellent reputation.

16. John, Frank, and Jim are all excellent students, but the former is almost unique in his ability to grasp new and difficult ideas.

17. His injury, which was due to a bad fall, forced him to lay in bed for an entire month.

18. She was adverse to being introduced as an alumna of a very inferior girls' college.

19. The candidate adverted to a remark made by his opponent which mitigated against his chance of winning the election.

20. The children laid down there books on the sofa.

21. I implied from what he said that he was liable to be arrested.

22. He effected a great change in the morale of the employees by bringing coffee to their desks every morning.

23. He believed that he was likely to be honored due to his bravery.

24. The letter from the teacher implied that she was willing to learn her students any subject in the curriculum.

25. That kind of person is liable to become rich and famous because he is both talented and personable.

Answer Key

1 IDENTIFYING NOUNS

1. year
2. Marriage
3. place
4. result
5. art
6. fear
7. store
8. policemen
9. charity
10. nation
11. girl
12. advice
13. life
14. business
15. Thousands
16. comforts
17. dictation
18. sense
19. verdict
20. signers
21. work
22. trouble (2)
23. dance
24. wrench
25. work

2 IDENTIFYING NOUNS

1. Traffic — city
2. roads — concrete
3. John — breakfast
4. Haste — waste
5. lives — experience
6. Mary — brother
7. lights — room
8. exits — auditorium
9. noise — children
10. books — corridor
11. assignment — pages
12. hours — bus
13. programs — television
14. personality — actor
15. John — father
16. dogs — lunchroom
17. mists — night
18. deal — strength
19. teacher — class
20. child — street
21. friend — person
22. students — grades
23. car — place
24. book — floor
25. assignment — tools

3 IDENTIFYING AND CAPITALIZING PROPER NOUNS

1. Aunt Louise OR Louise
2. West
3. Sunday
4. New England
5. Quakers
6. The Purple Cow
7. Kurt Vonnegut
8. Mother
9. Italy
10. English
11. Father Wilson
12. Christmas
13. The Orpheum Theatre
14. Mexicans
15. Chicago
16. German
17. Fourteenth Street

18. The Outcasts Valley
19. Fourth July
20. Social Institutions
21. New York City

22. Thomas Jefferson High School
23. The Rewards Honesty
24. Judge Wilson
25. Mr. President

4 POSSESSIVE CASE OF NOUNS

1. The woman's dress
2. The women's club
3. The janitor's broom
4. The janitors' room
5. Hughes's novel
6. The secretary's chair
7. The bosses' suite
8. The ship's mast
9. The floor of the room
10. The airplane's gyroscope
11. John Abrams' essay
12. Dick and John's canoe
13. Dick's and John's sweaters

14. Shakespeare's works
15. The Smiths' house
16. The rails of the fence
17. Salter, Stone, and Atlas' firm
18. Salter's, Stone's, and Atlas' firms
19. Amos' books OR Amos's books
20. John's mother-in-law's ring
21. a three weeks' tour
22. seven dollars' worth
23. one hour's time
24. a two months' vacation
25. his money's worth

5 IDENTIFYING ANTECEDENTS OF PRONOUNS

1. senator
2. letter
3. Frederick
4. men
5. children
6. daughter
7. Money
8. man
9. people
10. The United Nations

11. plants
12. Mr. and Mrs. Johnson
13. Nobody
14. love
15. apples
16. We
17. women
18. Every adult OR adult
19. Jane or Louise

20. candidates
21. The United States
22. books and papers
23. little Susan OR Susan
24. The offensive linemen of the Jets OR The offensive linemen
25. Potatoes

6 CASE OF PRONOUNS

1. it
2. we
3. she
4. my OR mine
5. you
6. our OR ours
7. them
8. I
9. you
10. her
11. they
12. me
13. he
14. its
15. us
16. your
   OR yours
17. his
18. it
19. their OR
   theirs
20. him
21. her OR hers
22. who
23. whom
24. whose
25. whose

7 IDENTIFYING VERBS

1. was
2. devoted
3. waited
4. is
5. fought
6. sings
7. live
8. teach
9. meets
10. lasted
11. blew
12. had been blowing
13. will print
14. expected
15. have been waiting
16. was resting
17. will be seing
18. is setting
19. gasped
20. can expect
21. will have completed
22. was spent
23. has passed
24. was
25. do congratulate

8 TRANSITIVE AND INTRANSITIVE VERBS; VOICE AND MOOD OF VERBS

1. v.i.
2. v.i.
3. v.i.
4. v.t. bone
5. v.t. wrote
6. v.i.
7. v.t. plenty
8. v.t. "I do."
9. v.i.
10. v.i.
11. passive
12. passive
13. passive
14. passive
15. active
16. active
17. passive
18. active
19. imperative
20. indicative
21. subjunctive
22. indicative
23. subjunctive
24. imperative
25. subjunctive

9 CORRECT VERB FORMS

1. ate
2. shall take OR will take
3. was washing
4. will be seeing
5. was
6. had reached
7. had hoped
8. meets
9. audits
10. have been playing
11. had been waiting
12. shall have mended OR will have mended
13. are putting
14. shall do
15. will have been fighting
16. will leave
17. had been expecting
18. will attend
19. writes
20. have been planning

10 CORRECT FORMS OF IRREGULAR VERBS

1. bade
2. beat
3. borne
4. burst
5. cast
6. chose
7. clung
8. dealt
9. dived OR dove
10. drunk
11. fled
12. flew
13. flung
14. forbidden
15. hung
16. hanged
17. knelt
18. led
19. leaped OR leapt
20. lie
21. laying
22. lain
23. lying
24. laid
25. lay

11 CORRECT FORMS OF IRREGULAR VERBS

1. risen
2. run
3. sought
4. set
5. sits
6. set
7. sat
8. sank OR had sunk
9. slain
10. slung
11. slunk
12. spoken
13. stung
14. strode
15. sworn
16. swept
17. swum
18. swung
19. throve OR thrived
20. thrown
21. waked OR woken
22. worn
23. wept
24. wrung
25. written

12 IDENTIFYING ADJECTIVES

1. old / book
2. the / cashier
3. white / Americans
4. a / bill
5. tired / him
6. Lazy / he
7. an / orange
8. sick / dog
9. beautiful / picture
10. no / impression
11. famous / an
12. twenty / the
13. rich / famous
14. a / thinking

15. ready	sensible	21. Tired	hungry
16. better	cold	22. simple	enough
17. Sensitive	foolish	23. Medieval	shining
18. All	intrinsic	24. the	steel
19. an	old	25. uncomfortable	the
20. miserable	that		

13 IDENTIFYING ADVERBS

Word Modified	Part of Speech
1. happy	adj.
2. hummed	v.
3. walked	v.
4. studied	v.
5. ever	adv.
6. cold	adj.
7. tiptoed	v.
8. waited	v.
9. ready	adj.
10. goes	v.
11. pretty	adj.

12. home	early
13. hardly	ever
14. so	badly
15. never	late
16. slowly	deeply
17. Suddenly	not
18. slowly	silently
19. very	fast
20. very	unanimously
21. finally	up
22. almost	entirely
23. nearly	even
24. seemingly	finally
25. over	over

14 COMPARISON OF ADJECTIVES AND ADVERBS

1. prettier	prettiest
2. more miserable	most miserable
3. more quickly	most quickly
4. littler	littlest
5. worse	worst
6. better	best
7. more beautiful	most beautiful
8. more quietly	most quietly
9. more dignified	most dignified
10. more serene	most serene

11. taller
12. more rapidly
13. warmest
14. harder
15. most original
16. worse
17. best
18. more dignified
19. best
20. cheaper
21. quickest
22. more liberal
23. more sensible
24. richest
25. cheaper

15 CORRECT USE OF ADJECTIVES AND ADVERBS

1. hot	8. quiet	14. sweet	20. horrible
2. hot	9. quietly	15. quickly	21. well
3. bad	10. surely	16. wonderfully	22. terribly
4. good	11. somewhat	17. more easily	23. good
5. well	12. fiercely	18. suddenly	24. considerably
6. really	13. well	19. easily	25. smart
7. bad			

16 IDENTIFYING VERBALS

1. present infinitive	14. Knowing	gerund
2. present participle	15. reaching	gerund
3. past participle	16. screaming	gerund
4. present participle	17. screaming	
5. perfect infinitive	18. Convinced	
6. present perfect participle	19. daring	gerund
7. present participle	20. meeting	gerund
8. present participle	21. Having slept	
9. present infinitive	22. knowing	gerund
10. present infinitive	23. white-washed	
11. lending gerund	24. listening	gerund
12. told	25. laughing	gerund
13. fading		

17 POSSESSIVES BEFORE GERUNDS

1. John's	6. firm's	11. Caruso's	16. men's	21.
2.	7. class's	12. Frank's	17. women's	22. children's
3.	8. Mary's	13.	18.	23.
4. boys'	9. Johnson's	14. Mother's	19. witness's	24. Ruth's
5.	10.	15.	20. Ned's	25. Marshall's

18 IDENTIFYING CONJUNCTIONS AND PREPOSITIONS

		Preposition	Conjunction		Preposition	Conjunction
1. prep.	yesterday					
2. conj.						
3. conj.		11. for	and	19. by	that	
4. conj.		12. around	because	20. in	that	
5. conj.		13. for	When	21. before	if	
6. prep.	him	14. in	unless	22. by	that	
7. prep.	me	15. with	while	23. about	than	
8. conj.		16. in	and	24. like	or	
9. conj.		17. of	although	25. around	before	
10. prep.	store	18. into	whenever			

19 REVIEW: IDENTIFYING THE PARTS OF SPEECH

1. v.t.	9. v.t.	17. prep.	25. adv.	33. n.
2. adj.	10. adj.	18. adj.	26. conj.	34. prep.
3. n.	11. adj.	19. adj.	27. n.	35. adv.
4. adv.	12. n.	20. n.	28. n.	36. prep.
5. prep.	13. v.t.	21. adj.	29. v.t.	37. v.t.
6. adv.	14. conj.	22. adv.	30. adv.	38. n.
7. n.	15. conj.	23. v.t.	31. n.	39. adj.
8. prep.	16. n.	24. v.t.	32. v.i.	40. n.

20 IDENTIFYING SUBJECTS

1. neighbor	8. you (understood)	15. Basketball and handball
2. neighbor	9. journey	16. sports
3. Rent	10. planners	17. kinds
4. Rent and food	11. novel	18. food
5. he	12. lot	19. Neither John nor Jerry
6. reason	13. weeds	20. children
7. schedule	14. hat	

21 IDENTIFYING PREDICATES

1. break	11. is
2. put	12. was
3. checked and adjusted	13. had perfected
4. spent	14. plodded
5. Praise and pass	15. sat
6. Are running	16. was summoned and questioned
7. will have been serving	17. lay
8. married	18. lists
9. tried	19. betray and show
10. were governed	20. was

22 IDENTIFYING PHRASES

1. prep.	8. verb phrase	14. gerund	20. inf.
2. part.	9. prep.	15. prep.	21. verb phrase
3. prep.	10. inf.	16. prep.	22. prep.
4. verb phrase	11. gerund	17. prep.	23. prep.
5. inf.	12. verb phrase	18. part.	24. part.
6. gerund	13. part.	19. prep.	25. prep.
7. prep.			

23 IDENTIFYING INDEPENDENT CLAUSES

1. (He is the man)
2. (The director scolded)
   (the actors sulked.)
3. (During the seventeenth century, many actors achieved great fame)
   (they were not considered respectable members of society)
4. (you must take into account the annual temperature range in your area)
5. (Everyone knows)
6. (Eugenics is not a branch of natural science;)
   (it is a branch of social science.)
7. (Many animals can show that they are hungry,)
   (only man can ask for bread or an egg.)
8. (it is like a maze with many wrong turnings.)
9. (The scientific method refuses to ask questions)
10. (he attended many of its meetings.)
11. (the City Manager has not yet selected the agency to handle the loan fund.)
12. (They felt)
13. (The silver dollar is favored on the West Coast,)
    (few of them appear elsewhere.)
14. (hospitals long refused to accept unions and collective bargaining.)
15. (Mozart)
    (died young.)
16. (It has been said,)
    (the point appears in this article,)
17. (he shows himself to be a reactionary in the most formal sense of the term.)
18. (there will be love without marriage.)
19. (Who is so deaf)
20. (He thinks)
21. (the townspeople pull the shutters down over their shop windows and return to their homes.)
22. (We hoped)
23. (there would be more trouble in the world than there is now.)
24. (Jonathan Edwards,)
    (was an intellectual who devoted most of his great mental ability to the analysis and attempted solution of religious problems.)
25. (He did not try to avoid issues)

24 IDENTIFYING DEPENDENT CLAUSES

1. (that the war would end soon.)   noun
2. (before he had completed his last term of office.)   adverb
3. (who denied Jesus three times.)   adjective
4. (that an unexamined life is not worth living?)   noun
5. (who was an Afro-American member of Perry's
   expedition,)   adjective

6. (Because man's aggressiveness can be canalized into other outlets,)   adverb
7. (what William James called "a moral equivalent for war.")   noun
8. (As H.G. Wells said,)   adverb
9. (which is entirely dependent on timber.)   adjective
10. (that Darwin has been called the Newton of biology.)   noun
11. (Once the brain reaches a certain complexity,)   adverb
12. (that the war must be supported.)   noun
13. (that a third of American married women were gainfully employed.)   noun
14. (that the number of its employees reached one million for the first time in 1979.)   noun
15. (which was founded in 1910,)   adjective
16. (while the iron is hot.)   adverb
17. (If wishes were horses,)   adverb
18. (Because he often secured agreement, or the appearance of it,)   adverb
19. (Although the election appeared to be lost,)   adverb
20. (who dances)   adjective

25 RECOGNIZING TYPES OF SENTENCES

1. simple
2. complex
3. complex
4. compound
5. complex
6. simple
7. compound-complex
8. simple
9. simple
10. complex
11. compound
12. simple
13. compound-complex
14. simple
15. complex
16. simple
17. compound
18. compound
19. simple
20. complex
21. complex
22. complex
23. compound-complex
24. simple
25. simple

26 RECOGNIZING SENTENCE FRAGMENTS

1. fragment
2. sentence
3. fragment
4. fragment
5. sentence
6. fragment
7. fragment
8. fragment
9. fragment
10. sentence
11. fragment
12. fragment
13. sentence
14. sentence
15. fragment
16. fragment
17. fragment
18. fragment
19. sentence
20. fragment
21. fragment
22. sentence
23. fragment
24. sentence
25. fragment

27 IDENTIFYING AND CORRECTING SENTENCE FRAGMENTS

1.	(That)	We	fragment
2.	(who)		fragment
3.	(When)	The	fragment
4.			sentence
5.	(Because)	Management	fragment
6.			sentence
7.	(Since)	The	fragment
8.	(Although)	Many	fragment
9.	(Because)		fragment
10.			sentence
11.	(that)		fragment
12.	(Provided that)	The	fragment
13.	(When)	The	fragment
14.			sentence
15.	(that)		fragment
16.	(that)		fragment
17.	(where)		fragment
18.	(which)		fragment
19.	(When)	The	fragment
20.			sentence
21.			sentence
22.	(Where)	My	fragment
23.	(who)		fragment
24.	(As)	Time	fragment
25.	(which)		fragment

28 IDENTIFYING AND COMPLETING SENTENCE FRAGMENTS

1.	The delegate from India was discussing	fragment
2.	He pitched. . .	fragment
3.		sentence
4.	The National Urban League was founded. . .	fragment
5.	Robert Frost was an. . .	fragment
6.	In 1949, the war was over. . .	fragment
7.	The clay jars still contained some. . .	fragment
8.		sentence
9.	Their white robes and cowls covered them. . .	fragment
10.	He told his. . .	fragment

29 IDENTIFYING AND COMPLETING SENTENCE FRAGMENTS

1.	fragment		6.	sentence
2.	sentence		7.	sentence
3.	fragment		8.	fragment
4.	fragment		9.	fragment
5.	fragment		10.	sentence

30 DETECTING COMMA FAULTS

1. CF	6. C	11. CF	16. CF	21. C
2. CF	7. CF	12. C	17. CF	22. CF
3. C	8. CF	13. CF	18. CF	23. CF
4. C	9. C	14. CF	19. C	24. C
5. CF	10. C	15. C	20. C	25. CF

31 PUNCTUATING INDEPENDENT CLAUSES

1. engineer;
2. year;
3. whistle,
4. stormy,
5. states;
6. school,
7. salesman,
8. Indians,
9. picture;
10. month,
11. appear;
12. pilgrimages;
13. popular;
14. excellent;
15. City,
16. native;
17. form,
18. excellent,
19. harmful;
20. tools;
21. players,
22. exaggeration;
23. comet;
24. 1682,
25. incandescent,

32 LOCATING DIVISION POINTS BETWEEN SENTENCES

2.	changed significantly since the last century. The aim of	The
4.	man. Education for women was almost unknown. Jane Austen	Education, Jane
8.	leges for nearly anyone. In addition to colleges which grant	In
11.	level. It has been estimated that two million American stu-	It
13.	these are in four-year technical institutions. Most of them	Most
14.	are enrolled in two-year junior or community colleges. The	The
16.	er cost. Tuition is free in many publicly supported insti-	Tuition
17.	tutions, and the college is within commuting distance. Many	Many
20.	ployment. A number of business firms will even pay part or	A
21.	all of the tuition of their employees. The demand for grad-	The
26.	policy. This means that any high school graduate may enter	This
27.	without taking entrance examinations. Some two-year colleges	Some
31.	last ten years. There are now more than a thousand of them	There
32.	in America. In most of them students may choose an entire-	In
34.	four-year college if their records are good. If they are	If
36.	with an appropriate degree. Many academic courses are open	Many
37.	to both kinds of students. Of those who have transferred	Of
38.	to a senior college, nearly all have been successful. An	An
41.	faculty's teaching ability. Most four-year colleges are like-	Most
42.	ly to be more interested in scholarly attainments. There is	There

33 LOCATING DIVISION POINTS BETWEEN SENTENCES

2. was one of the most exciting events of his life. In May   In
6. honored. When he received the cable announcement, he commented: When
11. *City* for Europe. It was that first voyage that provided   It
13. fame. His friend and biographer, Albert Bigelow Paine, went   His
14. to the ship to bid him good-bye. To Paine, Mark "seemed a   To
17. His wife, Olivia, had died in 1904. Her death was the   Her
20. Those aboard the S.S. *Minneapolis* saw a man who had lived   Those
27. *neapolis* seems to have been a pleasant one for Twain. Albert   Albert
34. "made a stronger appeal than ever. The years had robbed   The
36. replace them." As Twain expressed it, "I had reached the   As
38. to adopt some." Paine wrote that Twain "adopted several on   Paine

34 RECOGNIZING FUSED SENTENCES

1. struck __X__ my	fused	14. Day __X__ the	fused
2. foolishly __X__ he	fused	15. August __X__ in	fused
3.	correct	16. constantly __X__ six	fused
4. Canada __X__ it	fused	17.	correct
5.	correct	18.	correct
6. songs __X__ in	fused	19. food __X__ even	fused
7. eve __X__ he	fused	20.	correct
8. speak __X__ its	fused	21. husband __X__ when	fused
9. expensive __X__ for	fused	22. gradualism __X__ they	fused
10. book __X__ there	fused	23. surgery __X__ his	fused
11.	correct	24. of __X__ he	fused
12.	correct	25.	correct
13. singer __X__ he	fused		

35 REVIEW: SENTENCE FRAGMENT, FUSED SENTENCE, AND COMMA FAULT

1. C	6. Fused	11. CF	16. CF	21. C
2. Frag.	7. C	12. CF	17. Fused	22. CF
3. CF	8. CF	13. Frag.	18. C	23. C
4. Fused	9. C	14. Frag.	19. Frag.	24. Fused
5. Frag.	10. Fused	15. C	20. Frag.	25. C

36 DETECTING DISAGREEMENTS OF SUBJECT AND VERB

1.	(Neither)	is	14.	C
2.	(several)	have	15. (Neither)	has
3.	(Some)	have	16. (that)	were
4.	C		17. (islands.)	are
5.	C		18. (Twenty years)	is
6.	(joy)	is	19. C	
7.	(None) (have)	C OR has	20. (legion)	was
8.	(Two-thirds)	are	21. (problem)	is
9.	C		22. (men)	are
10.	(school)	was	23. (major)	was
11.	(policy) (contract)	has	24. C	
12.	(rhythm) (meter)	are	25. C	
13.	C			

37 MAKING THE SUBJECT AND VERB AGREE

1.	selection	has	14. pleasure	was
2.	economics	does	15. dresses	were
3.	Allison, Twist and Turner, Inc.	was	16. refund	covers
4.	vestrymen	don't	17. president nor his advisors	have
5.	who	were	18. cloth or the dyes	are
6.	reasons	are	19. Every tree and every shrub	has
7.	Eight percent	is	20. band	is
8.	half	Has	21. miners	are
9.	wages	is	22. kinds	are
10.	wages	have	23. Some	is
11.	news	Is	24. Most	are
12.	team	were	25. reasons	are
13.	children	are		

38 MAKING THE SUBJECT AND VERB AGREE

1.	council	holds	13. supervisor and several	have
2.	objections	have	14. supervisor	has
3.	President	takes	15. Perkins and Company or Paul Fleischer Associates	Has
4.	statistics	is		
5.	knowledge	is	16. wife, mother and career woman	is
6.	Each	is	17. Exceptions	are
7.	package	is	18. test	is
8.	One	is	19. bus	does
9.	Which	has	20. mumps	is
10.	soldiers and sailors	lie		
11.	Most	have		
12.	All	are		

39 AGREEMENT OF PRONOUN AND ANTECEDENT

1. his or her
2. their
3. their
4. their
5. her
6. its
7. her
8. his
9. their
10. its
11. his
12. it
13. he
14. himself
15. its
16. its
17. its
18. them
19. his
20. he
21. their
22. he
23. its
24. it
25. he or she

40 AGREEMENT OF PRONOUN AND ANTECEDENT

1. their
2. their
3. their
4. his
5. their
6. his
7. their
8. its
9. its
10. her
11. its
12. your
13. its
14. his
15. their
16. her
17. her
18. his
19. it
20. his
21. her
22. their
23. its
24. his
25. her   her

41 CORRECTING DISAGREEMENTS OF PRONOUN AND ANTECEDENT

1. (Both)   their
2. (Each)   her
3. (coach nor the trainer)   his
4. (Anyone)   his or her
5. (speakers nor the moderator)   his
6. (Both Mr. Carstairs and Mr. Wilkins)   their
7. (Neither Mrs. Carstairs nor Mrs. Wilkins)   her
8. (Time)   its
9. (animal)   its
10. (man)   his
11. (Man)   him
12. (wealth nor a good reputation)   its
13. (staff)   its
14. (staff)   their
15. (faculty)   its
16. (Alice and Mary)   their
17. (problems)   them
18. (sublime and the ridiculous)   them
19. (men)   their
20. (The Bobbsey Twins)   it
21. (man)   his
22. (family)   its
23. (doors, guards, trappings)   they
24. (copy)   it
25. (employees)   their

42 CORRECTING DISAGREEMENTS OF PRONOUN AND ANTECEDENT

1. (authors and thinkers)   they
2. (man)   his
3. (History)   itself
4. (hen)   her
5. (Fortune)   she
6. (friends)   they
7. (actor)   him
8. (Pied Piper)   him
9. (aesthetics)   it
10. (economics)   it

11. (either Mrs. Cook or Mrs. Werbell)	her
12. (Company B)	its
13. (Channel 13)	its
14. (All students)	their
15. (Doctors)	they
16. (all Tuscarora Indians)	their
17. (Those who are)	themselves
18. (Lawyers)	their
19. (Job applicants)	their
20. (Parents)	their

43 IDENTIFYING PRONOUNS AND ANTECEDENTS

1.	he	vague	14.	which	vague
2.	who	man	15.	that	bindings
3.	which	trail	16.	who	landlord
4.	who	agent	17.	these	Bible, Schoolmen, Fathers, church councils
5.	his	craftsman			
6.	he	man	18.	that	sins
7.	which	vague	19.	its	teaching
8.	they	hailstones	20.	this	vague
9.	that	vague	21.	he	vague
10.	its	dog	22.	they	children
11.	who	Lewis Carroll	23.	that	figure of speech
12.	their	boys and girls	24.	that	novel
13.	who	relatives	25.	which	vague

44 IDENTIFYING PRONOUNS AND ANTECEDENTS

1.	it	company	11.	he	Merino
2.	their	picnickers	12.	they	lilies
3.	which	vague	13.	he	man
4.	he	vague	14.	this	vague
5.	who	people	15.	he	vague
6.	whom	attorney	16.	it	commercial
7.	which	vague	17.	he	Charles Lamb
8.	his	vague	18.	whom	leader
9.	who	commuters	19.	who	one
10.	he	vague	20.	it	vague

45 CASE OF NOUNS AND PRONOUNS

1. they
2. I
3. we
4. her
5. us
6. me
7. them
8. them
9. them
10. she
11. me
12. I
13. I
14. me
15. me
16. us
17. Whom
18. Who
19. Who
20. Whom
21. me
22. somebody's
23. somebody
24. Who
25. whom

46 CASE OF NOUNS AND PRONOUNS

1. girl
2. they
3. him
4. pity's
5. John's
6. John
7. I
8. I
9. him
10. we
11. His
12. him
13. I
14. I
15. Whom
16. Whom
17. Whom
18. Who
19. whoever
20. husband's
21. bird
22. dog's
23. dog
24. I
25. they

47 CORRECTING ERRORS IN CASE

1. (whom) who
2. (Henry) Henry's
3. (us) our
4. C
5. C
6. (I) me
7. (I) me
8. (I) me
9. C
10. (her) she
11. (who) whom
12. C
13. (them.) they
14. (them.) they
15. C
16. C
17. (I) me
18. (we) us
19. C
20. C
21. (Mary) Mary's
22. (I) me
23. (she) her
24. (me) I
25. (him) he

48 CORRECTING ERRORS IN CASE

1.	(us)	we		14.	C	
2.	C			15.	(Whom)	Who
3.	(us)	we		16.	(whom)	who
4.	C			17.	C	
5.	(me)	I		18.	C	
6.	(them)	they		19.	(us)	we
7.	C			20.	C	
8.	(they)	them		21.	C	
9.	(they)	them		22.	C	
10.	(us)	we		23.	(I)	me
11.	(us)	we		24.	(we)	us
12.	C			25.	(me)	I
13.	C					

49 DETECTING DANGLING MODIFIERS

1. (To be tender and digestible)   D
2. (To become a law)   D
3. C
4. C
5. (After serving in the Senate for sixteen years,)   D
6. C
7. (By scrimping and saving for five years,)   D
8. C
9. (To hook a rug)   D
10. (While representing the Apex Corporation in Rome,)   D
11. C
12. (After failing for years,)   D
13. (Lowering the shades,)   D
14. (Having been convicted of drunken driving,)   D
15. (By providing his own power line,)   D
16. (As the greatest golfer of all,)   D
17. (By using animated cartoons and other visual aids,)   D
18. (Upon learning that I was ill in the hospital,)   D
19. C
20. (In diagnosing certain illnesses,)   D
21. (Being an alien,)   D
22. (While driving through the Southwest,)   D
23. C
24. (In order to teach a person,)   D
25. (after working for days,)   D

50 CORRECTING DANGLING MODIFIERS

1. (To be mellow and subtle in taste,)
2. (To be sweet and mild,)
3. (While searching through bundles of unclassified periodicals in the Library of Congress,)
4. (while looking at me sorrowfully,)
5. (In order to sell a man insurance,)
6. (In comparing these two hearing aids,)
7. (Though musical and facile at the piano,)
8. (While painting Guernica,)
9. (To receive a reply to your inquiry,)
10. (By comparing these two specimens under the microscope,)
11. (Born and raised in Ireland,)
12. (from smoking too many cigarettes.)
13. (Played with exquisite musicianship,)
14. (To get a passport,)
15. (Holding two full-time jobs,)
16. (Reading the poetry of Dylan Thomas,)
17. (by granting credit too readily.)
18. (Though replete with beautiful passages and well-conceived characters,)
19. (While learning to play tennis as a boy,)
20. (In order to be an entertainer,)

51 MISPLACED MODIFIERS

1.	(when he was a boy.)	Kevin
2.	(almost)	a
3.	(in a shrill voice.)	He
4.	(on the advice of his doctor)	E
5.	(only)	the
6.	(with a solicitous and courtly air.)	Disraeli
7.	(almost)	a
8.	(only)	virtue
9.	(merely)	for
10.	(chiefly)	obliterated
11.	(that evening)	The
12.	(no doubt)	His
13.	(though divided)	has
14.	(after attending the institute for a semester.)	He
15.	(within a week)	E
16.	(before his pen had gleaned his teeming brain)	E
17.	(based on his personal experience.)	of
18.	(within two years)	E
19.	(only)	One
20.	(only)	one

52 DETECTING MIXED AND SPLIT CONSTRUCTIONS

1. M	6. C	11. S	16. S	21. S
2. M	7. C	12. M	17. C	22. C
3. M	8. S	13. C	18. C	23. C
4. M	9. S	14. C	19. M	24. M
5. C	10. S	15. M	20. M	25. S

53 DETECTING SPLIT CONSTRUCTIONS

1. (fluently)	split	
2. (quickly)	split	
3. (deeply)	split	
4. C		
5. (no doubt)	split	
6. (in our childhood)	split	
7. (in the duodenal region)	split	
8. (with a discreet cough,)	split	
9. (your salesman promised,)	split	
10. C		
11. (into law)	split	
12. (as I knew they would,)	split	
13. (as our enemies know,)	split	
14. (when the stock market crashed)	C	

15. (who would recommend our present course of defense) — split
16. (to everybody's surprise) — split
17. (in that remote section of Utah) — split
18. (by his afflictions and his comforters) — split
19. C
20. (in their nakedness,) — split
21. (in this unexplored wilderness) — split
22. (at once) — split
23. (as every schoolboy knows,) — split
24. C
25. (with a burst of scoring in the final minutes) — split

54 DETECTING INCOMPLETE AND ILLOGICAL COMPARISONS

1. W	6. W	11. C	16. C	21. W
2. W	7. C	12. W	17. W	22. W
3. C	8. C	13. W	18. W	23. C
4. C	9. W	14. W	19. W	24. W
5. W	10. C	15. C	20. W	25. C

55 INCOMPLETE AND ILLOGICAL COMPARISONS

1. as	6. he liked OR did	11. of any
2. other	7. those of	12. C
3. other	8. other	13. larger
4. C	9. C	14. tallest
5. of	10. C	15. better

16. C
17. of any
18. other
19. other
20. those in

21. of OR Franklin Roosevelt did
22. she trusted OR Gladstone did
23. C
24. they were
25. best

56 SUPPLYING NECESSARY WORDS

1. C
2. I OR He OR She, the, a, the
3. C
4. C
5. A
6. A
7. C
8. C
9. C
10. C
11. been
12. on OR C
13. A

14. is OR was OR will be
15. were
16. is
17. was
18. C
19. A
20. that
21. been
22. that
23. were
24. an
25. C

57 NECESSARY WORDS AND INCOMPLETE CONSTRUCTIONS

11. his
12. complete
13. in
14. in
15. that
16. is
17. that
18. the

19. his
20. the
21. the
22. his
23. earned
24. the
25. an

58 PARALLELISM

1. X	6. C	11. X	16. C
2. C	7. C	12. X	17. X
3. C	8. X	13. C	18. C
4. X	9. X	14. X	19. X
5. X	10. C	15. X	20. X

59 CONSISTENCY

1. Its	6. you
2. discover	7. his
3. others	8. jumped
4. they	9. they
5. they reproduce	10. explained

60 TERMINAL PUNCTUATION

1. ?	6. !	11. ?	16. ?	21. ?
2. !	7. period	12. period	17. !	22. ?
3. period	8. ?	13. period	18. period	23. ?
4. period	9. period	14. period	19. period	24. period
5. period	10. !	15. period	20. !	25. ?

61 THE COMMA: TO SEPARATE PARTS OF A SERIES

1. curb, looked about uncertainly,
6. worn-out, tiresome,
7. alphabet, the wheel, the sidewalk,
8. Company, Johnson's & West's,
9. thinking, fair in his dealings,
10. Wordsworth, Coleridge, Keats, Shelley,
11. brake, stepped on the gas,
12. work, knows how to relax,
13. exciting, the second act was interesting,
14. green, blue,
15. work, abortion on demand,
16. 1642, incorporated as a village in 1800,
19. watertight,
20. great, some achieve greatness,
23. Maryland, made nineteen trips south,
24. Vermont, New Hampshire, Massachusetts, Maine, Rhode Island,
25. punched, kicked, scratched,

62 THE COMMA: TO SEPARATE CLAUSES OF A COMPOUND SENTENCE JOINED BY A COORDINATING CONJUNCTION

1.	6.	11. ,for	16. ,but
2. ,but	7. ,and	12. ,and	17.
3.	8. ,yet	13. ,yet	18. ,and
4. ,for	9. ,or	14. ,and	19.
5. ,but	10. ,nor	15. ,for	20. ,and

63 THE COMMA: TO SEPARATE NON-INTEGRATED SENTENCE ELEMENTS

1. late,
2. Yes,
3. dates,   girl,
4. insisted,   moreover,
5. way,
6. Nonsense,
7. fork,   Edna,
8. confident,   ripe,
9. Consequently,
10. me,   Hudson
11. No,
12. obvious,   are,
13. here,   Doctor,

14. long,   however,
15. Anyway,
16. Well,
17. Oh,
18. know,   sake,
19. Tomlison,
20. favorable,
21. President,
22. that,
23. place,
24. Altogether,
25. me,

64 THE COMMA: TO SET OFF A LONG PHRASE OR CLAUSE PRECEDING THE SUBJECT

1. organizations,
2.
3.
4. teeth,
5.
6. time,
7. letter,
8. river,
9. car,
10.
11. us,
12.
13.

14. books,
15. grandfather,
16.
17.
18. game,
19.
20. 7th,
21. afternoon,
22.
23.
24. store,
25. decision,

65 THE COMMA: TO INDICATE INTERRUPTIONS OF NORMAL WORD ORDER

1. tribute,   clear,
2. clothes,   moth-eaten,
3. will,   sure,
4. graduates,   know,
5. name,   Christine,
6. Thomas,   one,
7. Congress,   reelection,
8. tempting,   discovered,
9. month,   April,
10. secretary,   reliable,
11.
12. Eleanor,   fancy-free
13. John,   was,
14. that,   most,
15. philosopher,   Montaigne,
16.
17.
18. shore,   heard,
19. time,   you,
20. responsibility,   responsibility,

66 THE COMMA: TO SET OFF NONRESTRICTIVE ELEMENTS

2. patients,		13. Express,	for,
5. Frazer,	cartels,	15. plays,	Hamlet,
6. Frost,	poet,	17. Orleans,	
9. Glade,		20. poem,	Aeneid,
11. words,	martinet,		

67 THE COMMA: TO EMPHASIZE CONTRAST AND TO PREVENT MISREADING

1. find,	6. Jim	11. good,	16. rained,	21. met,
2. state,	7. around,	12. pitched,	17. to,	22. up,
3. happy,	8. project,	13. once,	18. success,	23. year,
4. only,	9. pleasure,	14. children,	19. over,	24. sung,
5. Beneath,	10. all,	15. company,	20. fancy,	25. president, congress,

68 REVIEW: THE COMMA

1. forgotten,	25. scholars,
3. meaning, example, eye,	26. phrase,
4. swoop, berry, teeth,	27. Chaucer,
12. apple,	28. however,
14. me,	29. Chaucer, spelling,
17. about, him,	33. method, become, unaccountably,
23. blackberries,	34. event, appropriate, not,
24. raspberries, blueberries, hue,	35. mulberry, blueberry,

69 THE SEMICOLON

1.	6. hill;	
2. Joan;	7. politics;	
3. feet;	8. judgment;	
4. sense;	9. policy;	
5. foot;	10. inning;	second;

70 THE COLON, THE DASH, THE HYPHEN

1. band:
2. lodge—   invited—
3. I—   you—
4. follows:
5. him:
6.
7. society:
8. states:
9.
10. assignment—   better—

11. re-echo
12. yellow-green
13.
14. re-create
15. lighter-than-air
16. Yale-Harvard
17. dyed-in-the-wool
18. twenty-three
19. well-lighted
20. anti-intellectual

71 QUOTATION MARKS

1.   expenses,"
2. "It
3. "That   organization,"   "is   carefully."
4. "hanged   dead."
5. "The   Mississippi"
6.
7. "Didn't   'Keep   happens' "?
8. "The   People";
9. "America   America"?
10. "I   it?"
11. "What   Future?"
12. "It   useless,"   "to   them."
13. "Pull   fire,"   "Are   friends?"
14. "What   Know?"
15. "It's   future,"
16. "Can   'Home   Home'?"
17. "Save   me!"
18.
19. "I   much":
20. "Don't   'I'm stupid'!"

72 ITALICS AND QUOTATION MARKS TO INDICATE TITLES

1. *War and Peace*?
2.
3. *London Times*
4. "Take Care of Your Heart"
5. "The Raven"
6. "Ode to the West Wind"
7.
8. *Lohengrin*
9.
10. *The Literary Digest*.
11. "The Lexicographer's Easy Chair."
12. "Changing Conditions"
13. *The School for Scandal*

14. *Aeneid*
15. *The English Poets*.
16.
17. "The Star-Spangled Banner."
18. "Twenty Years from Now"
19. *Tom Jones*
20.
21.
22.
23. "Americana."
24. *Gone With the Wind*
25. "A Dissertation upon Roast Pig"

73 PUNCTUATION: REVIEW (1)

Sections 25, 26, 27, 28, 29, 30, 31, 34, 35, *Essentials of English*

Punctuate the following exercises, adding all needed punctuation, including quotation marks and italics.

EXAMPLE:

John my oldest brother said that he had read Shakespeare's Othello with great pleasure It taught me a lot about jealousy he said

PUNCTUATED: John, my oldest brother, said that he had read Shakespeare's Othello with great pleasure. "It taught me a lot about jealousy," he said.

1. He took his club in his hand, and with it he struck a stag such a great blow that he brayed vehemently, and at his braying the animals came flocking as numerous as the stars in the sky,—so rapidly that before I could ask, "What are you doing that for?" the glade was packed solid with woodland creatures.

2. There were openings for five stenographers, two typists, and four filing clerks in the shipping department; three secretaries, six copy-writers, and four layout men in the advertising department; and two accountants and five bookkeepers in the controller's office.

3. John Miles sent his short story "The Open Door" to The Little Magazine. "Devil take them!" he raged when it was rejected. "I'll bet," he added wryly, "the editor would have rejected 'The Outcasts of Poker Flat' if he had never heard of Bret Harte as a famous writer of short stories."

4. To Whom It May Concern: This is to certify that Mary Smith has been employed by this firm for the past ten years and has always been efficient, cooperative, and diligent in every way.

5. "This is an unlooked-for and unhoped-for honor, my friends," said my uncle when he was given a party in honor of his eighty-first birthday. "Anyone who has lived as long as I have," he continued, "is lucky to have any friends left, and I am sure we all ask ourselves, 'How many more years shall we be among the living?'"

6. The following committee members were present at the meeting: Edward Jones, Frank Simmons, Anna Metcalf, Leslie Hall, and Janet Fox.

7. After a long, hot, dusty ride on what must have been the oldest daycoach on the railroad, my friend Bob finally exploded. "Never again!" he roared. "John, if you ever ask me—and I mean it—to go anywhere with you again, see to it that you pick a cool day and a pleasanter means of transportation."

8. On a never-to-be-forgotten day in early August, we arrived in Mexico City. The weather was perfect, the hotel reservation was paid for, and we were ready to enjoy the first real vacation we had had in twenty-three years.

9. Ernest Hemingway, the celebrated American author, took his title for his novel The Sun Also Rises from the Biblical book of Ecclesiastes. The title is effective in itself; however, it is more meaningful if one is aware of the entire passage from which it was taken—not to mention the generally pessimistic and gloomy outlook conveyed by the entire book.

10. The rains having come early, we anticipated an excellent crop that year; furthermore, we had plowed deeply, fertilized well, and sowed the finest seed.

74 PUNCTUATION: REVIEW (2)

Sections 25, 26, 27, 28, 29, 30, 31, 34, 35, *Essentials of English*

Punctuate the following exercises, adding all needed punctuation, including quotation marks and italics.

EXAMPLE:

John my oldest brother said that he had read Shakespeare's Othello with great pleasure It taught me a lot about jealousy he said

PUNCTUATED: John, my oldest brother, said that he had read Shakespeare's *Othello* with great pleasure. "It taught me a lot about jealousy," he said.

1. When my uncle took his family on a summer vacation in Maine, he complained about the weather, the prices, and the food. When he took his family on a winter vacation in Florida, he complained about the weather, the prices, and the food. My aunt plans to take a vacation by herself next year! or .

2. At the world-famous battle of Marathon, the disposition of the Greek forces was as follows: the right wing was led by Callimachus, the center was divided among the other leaders of the Athenians, and the left wing was formed by the Plataeans. When the Persians advanced in full battle array, the Athenians in the center charged them at full speed. The Persians thought that the Greeks were out of their minds, for they saw a mere handful of men coming at them. While this small force was engaging the Persians, however, the two Greek wings converged upon the center, fought the enemy valiantly, and completely routed them.

3. In his essay On "Flattery," one of the thirty character sketches that make up the work known as The Moral Characters, Theophrastus states, "Flattery is a base manner of conversation that tends only to the advantage of the flatterer." He goes on to describe the many things a flatterer does to make himself agreeable to everybody he meets. He concludes by saying, "In short, the flatterer has but one design in all his words and actions, and that is to catch men by their weak side and to ingratiate himself into their favor."

4.   John and Mary were driving down a long, narrow, bumpy country road on the way to visit John's cousin. "Will you try to like her?" said John. "She is a very easy-to-get-along-with kind of person."

"How old is she?" asked Mary.

"She must be—let's see—why, she must be twenty-one by now. How time flies! It seems only yesterday that she was a little girl in pigtails reciting 'Mary, Mary, Quite Contrary' and singing—I'll never forget it—'The Farmer in the Dell' in a funny, high, squeaky baby voice."

5. The men who came to Independence Hall to volunteer their services were angry when they were informed that they were not needed, although there was really no reason for them to be annoyed.

6. "I see by The New York Times," said Mother, "that the prices keep right on going up. Don't tell Father. He will only say, 'Don't you know that prices go only one way-up?'"

7. The room was furnished handsomely, not elaborately; moreover, everything about it bespoke the exquisite taste of the owner.

8. The old oak tree, gnarled and majestic, dominated the lawn; other trees seemed puny by comparison.

75 WRITING PARAGRAPHS
(Sample answers)

A. 1. From the first to the third grade, my experiences with the opposite sex were innocent and uninhibited. On my first day at school, a lovely little girl tossed her volleyball to me, and we played catch on the playground at recess. In the second grade I had a crush on my teacher, an aging lady who was all of thirty years old. This great romance left me with little emotion for the girls of my own age, but we continued to chase each other on the playground. In the third grade I began to feel the first intimations that those students who wore dresses and had long pigtails were somehow different. We didn't stop chasing each other on the playground, but somehow I began to suspect that the chasing had a deeper meaning.

2. The best way to describe Picasso's painting *Guernica* is to go from left to right on his canvas. The eye usually enters a painting on the left, and in this case, we first see a woman with an elongated neck holding the body of a dead child. Just above these two is a bull whose buttocks and tail resemble an abstract volcanic mountain in eruption. Next in order is a large woman, prone on her back, looking like a fallen statue, perhaps of justice. Above her is a horse with neck painfully awry, and above the horse is an ovate sun, with an incandescent bulb in the center. Just to the right is the head of what appears to be a godlike creature—like the god of the wind—and he is holding a lamp. Further to the right is a figure with hands upraised in horror as an object falls from the heavens, like a bomb. The painting is horrible to behold because it shows so graphically the horrors of war.

B. 1. In evaluating my use of time, I like to list everything I do in a day in a rank of ascending importance. Perhaps the least important things I do—although they are necessary for life—are taking care of the physical needs of my body. In this category are routine things like taking a shower, brushing my teeth, and eating my three meals. The next category in an ascending order of importance deals with the improvement of my mind, and this includes reading a newspaper, becoming informed on further events of the day by watching television news, and studying for all of my classes. Even more important is staying alert and listening to what my teachers say in class. The most important things I do each day are those actions that improve my relationships with those around me, as I try to understand and get along well with my family, my friends, and all the people with whom I am associated on the journey of life.

2. Thurman Munson was valuable to the New York Yankees in a great many ways. He was a great batter who could be depended on to get the crucial hit and drive in the much-needed run when the team was behind in late innings. He was an outstanding defensive catcher, who rarely let anything get by him at the plate. He had a strong arm, which was respected around the league by those who might want to steal bases. But most of all, he was a team leader. He inspired his fellow players and led them to play even better than they knew they could.

76 DEVELOPING PARAGRAPHS
(Sample answers)

A. 1. My bedroom is a reflection of my personality. I like sports, and many of the objects in the room show that interest. There are two tennis rackets, along with a can of balls, in one corner. On a shelf above them is a trophy I won last summer at camp, when I was runner up in the tennis tournament for my age group. Peeking out from under the bed is a football helmet and the toes of a pair of football shoes. I play on the junior high team as a wide receiver, and I often practice in the park with a friend of mine who happens to be a quarterback and throws the ball well. On the wall is my collection of baseball cards, and I have all of the Yankees and the Mets for the last ten years, all taped to my wall just above my bed. Anyone visiting my bedroom would think I am a sports nut. I am.

2. Professional sports and high school athletics are different in many ways and similar in only a few points. First of all, the professionals are bigger, faster, and certainly wealthier. Now that such tremendous salaries are being paid to professional athletes, more and more people are competing for the few possible slots on the teams, and this results in a highly selective competition, with only the most highly qualified athletes making the team. In high school, where the coach can choose only from students in the school, he must do the best he can with the talent available. Though the professionals and the high school athletes play the same game, football, and though they run, block, kick, and tackle in somewhat the same way, the superior talents and abilities of the professionals make it almost seem to be a different game.

B. 1. When people are idle, bored, or frustrated, trouble often develops. The next time you are with a group of people for a long period, notice that relationships tend to be good when everyone is just beginning the day with routine tasks to be done. People are in good spirits and well rested. Later in the day, as blood sugar gets low, weariness sets in, and the later tasks become boring or frustrating. It is then that nerve ends get raw, and people begin to get under each other's skins. At this point, beware of trouble.

2. Courage can have many different aspects in various situations. When we think of courage, we often limit ourselves to war heroes, but there are many women who show courage off the battlefield. Joan of Arc died courageously as she was burned at the stake, breathing a forgiving prayer for her accusers. And there are many less dramatic examples of courage: Elizabeth Blackwell completing her medical education and becoming the first woman doctor, Susan B. Anthony campaigning for women's right to vote, Jeanette Rankin of Montana becoming the first woman in Congress, even before women could vote nationwide.

77 USING TRANSITIONAL EXPRESSIONS FOR PARAGRAPH COHERENCE

1.	In fact	emphasis	14.	accordingly	result
2.	indeed	emphasis	15.	similarly	comparison
3.	for instance	example	16.	For this purpose	purpose
4.	For this purpose	purpose	17.	Moreover	addition
5.	after all	contrast	18.	finally	addition
6.	However	contrast	19.	in fact	emphasis
7.	likewise	comparison	20.	At the same time	time
8.	for example	example	21.		
9.	nevertheless	contrast	22.	To sum up	summary
10.	it is true	emphasis	23.		
11.	consequently	result	24.	yet	contrast
12.	indeed	emphasis	25.	on the other hand	contrast
13.	Furthermore	addition	26.		

78 MAKING PARAGRAPHS COHERENT (*Sample answer*)

There are many things that have to be done in order to plan a successful vacation trip to Europe. First of all, read travel books so that you will know where to go to get the maximum value from your trip. Learn what months are best for good weather; rainy, cold days can ruin a vacation trip. Very early in your planning, decide where you want to go, and how long you will stay in each place. This will enable you to find the least expensive round-trip flights and purchase your tickets ahead of time. Buy a book that lists accommodations and good sight-seeing areas, and reserve rooms in centrally located, moderately priced hotels or guest houses. Also, in order to plan your ground transportation abroad, learn about the Eurail pass, and determine from maps showing your itinerary whether or not the pass will be better than buying each separate railway ticket. As the time for your trip approaches, get a book that has the basic foreign language phrases you will need, and practice saying them. Learn something about the history of the countries so that what you see will be meaningful. Most important of all, pack carefully, and take as little luggage as possible.

79 LIMITING THE SUBJECT (*Sample answers*)

1. The Role of Working Mothers	definition
2. A Day in the Life of an Honest Person	modes of operation
3. Droughts Cause Most Famines	cause and effect
4. Political Power in the White House Staff	organization
5. Throwing the Short Pass	component parts
6. Cold Fronts vs. Warm Fronts Lead to Tornadoes.	cause and effect
7. Truth in Cigarette Advertising	definition
8. Wedding Ceremonies in Japan	place
9. The Organization of French Military Companies at the Battle of Waterloo	organization
10. How to Accept Substitute Motions	modes of operation

80 DETERMINING THE FUNDAMENTAL PURPOSE (*Sample answers*)

A. 1. What is freedom?

Purpose Statement One: I am writing this essay to show that freedom is a privilege that must be carefully guarded. To protect my freedom, I must help protect the freedom of others.

Purpose Statement Two: Freedom must be defined differently when a person is free only because he has nothing to lose; my purpose is to show that this kind of freedom is not really freedom.

2. The old man who sells papers near the subway entrance is interesting both in his mannerisms and his dress.

Purpose Statement One: My purpose is to choose details of description which show that I feel positively toward the old man.

Purpose Statement Two: My purpose in writing this is to be as objective as possible, showing both the positive and negative points about the old man.

3. A museum of natural history has many interesting things to delight the eye and stimulate the mind.

Purpose Statement One: I want to concentrate on details from exhibits that show the changing nature of human beings from prehistoric times to the present.

Purpose Statement Two: I want to concentrate on the earliest marine life on our planet.

B. 1. A funny thing happened to me on the way to class today.

Purpose Statement One: My purpose is to tell a story that is funny at my expense, making myself the butt of the joke.

Purpose Statement Two: I want to tell a funny story that pokes fun at another person.

2. Courage can have many different aspects in various situations.

Purpose Statement One: I want to write about examples of courage in the face of physical danger.

Purpose Statement Two: I want to show examples of day-to-day courage in facing life's problems.

3. The beginning of one's education in the first grade is like starting a journey.

Purpose Statement One: The purpose of this paper is to show the preparation that has led to one's arriving at school age, comparing this to preparing for a journey.

Purpose Statement Two: The purpose of this paper is to show that beginning school and beginning a journey are alike in that both have an impetus that carries one along, and both lead to uncertainties, since no one knows how the journey will end.

---

81 PLANNING YOUR WRITING (*Sample answers*)

I. *General Subject:* What Is Honesty?

Limited Subject: A Day in the Life of an Honest Person

Purpose Statement: My purpose is to present examples of the conduct of an honest person in two familiar settings.

Preliminary List of Ideas
1. At breakfast, truthfully tells parents plans for the day
2. Returns exact change to father for purchase made for him
3. At newspaper stand, is given too much change and returns it
4. Tells teacher she was unable to complete the assignment and gives honest reason
5. Tells little brother she does not approve of his whining
6. Tells friend at school tactfully that her hair needs cutting
7. Sees that the answer sheet of the smartest student in class is clearly visible during a test, but ignores it, without trying to read the answers
8. Is asked her opinion on the site chosen for the Junior-Senior Dance, and she gives it honestly even though her statement is unpopular
9. Finds a quarter on the street
10. Plans to write a paper on honesty

11. Remembers being embarrassed as a child when she was honest about her aunt's new dress
12. Finds library book on a bench and returns it to the school library

Elimination of ideas that do not fit: #3, #9, #10, and #11.

Topic Outline

I. The honest person at home
   A. #1
   B. #2
   C. #5

II. The honest person at school
   A. #12
   B. #4
   C. #7
   D. #6
   E. #8

(Notice: This outline may seem overly simple to you, but experience has proved that the simplest outlines are best.)

II. *General Subject:* The Roles of Males and Females: Cave Man to Modern Man

Limited Subject: The Role of Working Mothers

Purpose Statement: My purpose is to create a positive impression of a mother as she performs in three different roles.

Preliminary List of Ideas
Working mothers
   1. cook meals
   2. comfort children
   3. wash and dry clothes
   4. act as nurses for sick children
   5. make decisions at work
   6. prepare budgets for their departments at work
   7. plan budgets for their homes
   8. help with homework
   9. confer with their bosses
   10. call repairmen if appliances at home break down
   11. discuss work deficiencies with employees
   12. discuss school deficiencies with children
   13. go on vacations
   14. like to watch soap operas, but cannot
   15. do not like fast food restaurants

Elimination of ideas that do not fit: #13, #14, and #15.

Topic Outline

I. The Working Mother as Homemaker
   A. #1
   B. #3
   C. #7
   D. #10

II. The Working Mother as Mother
   A. #2
   B. #4
   C. #12

III. The Working Mother as Business Executive
   A. #5
   B. #6
   C. #9
   D. #11

---

82 STANDARD ABBREVIATIONS

1. anon.
2. bks.
3. ca. OR c.
4. ch. 4
5. col. 2
6. ed.
7. e.g.
8. et al.
9. p. 19f
10. p. 19ff
11. ibid., OR ib. OR id. OR idem
12. i.e.
13. ll.
14. ms. OR ms OR MS. or MS
15. loc. cit.
16. N.B. or n.b.
17. n.d.
18. n.p.
19. pp.
20. par.
21. passim
22. sic
23. trans. OR tr.
24. viz.
25. vol.

83 FOOTNOTE TECHNIQUES

1. James Nelson, *Myths of the Orient* (Chicago: Norris, Page, & Smith, 1848), II, 47–49.
2. Sanford Wallis, "Trade and Manufacturing," *Dominant Aspects of the American Economy*, ed. Russell Ford (Boston: Grant & Norcross, 1960), p. 216.
3. Jean Reynard, *Paris*, trans. Lester Kirk (London: James Hyman, n.d.), pp. 7–12.
4. Ibid., p. 217.
5. Joshua Small, "Is Cotton Still King?" The New Orleans *Bugle* (October 17, 1903), Sec. 1, p. 2.
6. Ibid.
7. Victor Harris and Frank Stallman, "Trends and Tendencies in Advertising," *Selling* (April, 1940), p. 67.
8. *Paris*, p. 119. OR Reynard, p. 119.
9. J. Miles Prendergast, Dukes and Dutchesses (sic) (n.p., n.d.), pp. 74–79.
10. "John Bunyan," *Encyclopedia Brittanica*, 11th ed., III, 94.

84 FOOTNOTE AND BIBLIOGRAPHY TECHNIQUES (Directions)

1. Clifford Matthews, "Louise," *Tales of the Sea*, ed. Searle Weeks and Mary Page, p. 14.
2. Sir Richard Falkland, *Ships of His Majesty's Navy*, II, 19–21.
3. Ibid., I, 217.
4. Ibid.
5. *Complete Shipping Guide*, p. 127.
6. "Louise," p. 17. OR Matthews, p. 17.
7. John Baumgartner and Heinrich Zeller, "Viking Ship Construction," *Master Builders of the Sea*, p. 24.
8. Sir Richard Falkland, *Sea Fortresses*, p. 10.
9. Margot Sanders, "Irridescence," 1. 17.
10. Ibid., 11. 27–29.

BIBLIOGRAPHY

Complete Shipping Guide. San Francisco: Stuart, Ross, & Co., 1918.

Baumgartner, Johann and Zeller, Heinrich, "Viking Ship Construction," Trans. Edna Morse, in Wilmot, Francis and Parker, Nelson, *Master Builders of the Sea*, n.p., 1903.

Falkland, Sir Richard, *Sea Fortresses*. London: Lindsey Heath, 1865.

—*Ships of his Majesty's Navy*, 3 vols. London: Nelson Briscoe, 1860.

Matthews, "Louise," in Weeks, Searle and Page, Mary, eds., *Tales of the Sea*. Dublin: John O'Neill, 1940.

Sanders, Mary, "Irridescence." *Sand and Spray*, Vol. 17, No. 2, spring, 1916.

85 CORRECTING MISUSED WORDS AND PHRASES

1. had ought
2. A person
3. counsel
4. woman
5. whose
6. an
7. proceeded
8. doesn't
9. that

10. all right
11. Fewer
12. Therefore
13. it's
14. number
15. principal
16. first OR first named
17. lie

18. averse
19. militated
20. their
21. Inferred
22. taking
23. because of
24. teach
25. likely

Notes

Notes